THE

God

OF THE
TOWEL

Other books by Jim McGuiggan:

Jesus, Hero of Thy Soul
Where the Spirit of the Lord Is . . .

THE  God OF THE TOWEL

Knowing the Tender Heart of God

JIM MCGUIGGAN

HOWARD
PUBLISHING CO.
West Monroe, Louisiana

Our purpose at Howard Publishing is to:

- *Increase faith* in the hearts of growing Christians
- *Inspire holiness* in the lives of believers
- *Instill hope* in the hearts of struggling people
  everywhere

Because He's coming again!

The God of the Towel
© 1997 by Jim McGuiggan
All rights reserved

Published by Howard Publishing Co., Inc.,
3117 North 7th Street, West Monroe, LA 71291-2227

Printed in the United States of America
Third printing 1998

Library of congress Cataloging-in-Publication Data

McGuiggan, Jim, 1937-
    The God of the towel : knowing the tender heart of God / Jim McGuiggan.
      p. cm.
    Includes bibliographical references.
    ISBN 1-878990-63-2 (alk. paper)
    1. God—Love. I. Title.
BT140.M42 1997
231'.6—dc20   96-43931
                                      CIP

Cover Illustration by Joe Clark
Jacket Design by LinDee Loveland
Edited by Philis Boultinghouse

◆

DEDICATION

This book is for Imo.

CONTENTS

Introduction   *1*

CHAPTER ONE

THE GOD WHO LOVES HUMANS

A Vulnerable God   *7*
Why Would He Bother?   *11*
God's Loving Purpose   *15*
Cherishing the Mystery   *19*
Don't Give Up on Me!   *23*
This God Came to Die!   *25*
Love in Four Dimensions   *29*
A Love That Will Not Let Me Go   *33*

CHAPTER TWO

THE GOD WHO LOVES THE WEAK

Allowances   *39*
Sticking Up for the Underbird   *43*
Bruised Reeds and Smoking Wicks   *47*
Receiver of Wrecks   *51*
The Shepherd King   *55*
Where Are the Stretchers?   *59*

CHAPTER THREE

THE GOD WHO IS HOLY

A Love That Can Be Trusted *65*
God's Ethical Holiness *69*
More Than Pardon *73*
The Gift of Holiness *77*
"And Maddest of All . . ." *81*
The Loving Holiness of God *85*

CHAPTER FOUR

THE GOD WHO FORGIVES SINS

Forgiveness and Repentance *91*
If Our Hearts Condemn Us *95*
Isn't Somebody Going to Forgive Me? *99*
Of Judges and Friends *103*
Ruby Bridges *107*
Humans Need Forgiving *111*
God Delights in Forgiving! *113*
No Fishing! *117*
Jesus Paid It All! *121*
Why Must You Die? *123*

CHAPTER FIVE

THE GOD OF THE TOWEL

Twelve Lords, One Servant *127*
God Is Not Slumming *131*
With Love and Forethought *135*
The Lamb at the Center of the Throne *137*

Contents

♦

Power: Pagan and Christ-like   *139*
"Made a Difference to That One"   *143*
Take My Word for It   *145*
Only Half the Cure   *147*

CHAPTER SIX

THE GOD WHO ALLOWS SUFFERING

Hang Nails and Colon Cancers   *151*
Can You Still Trust Me?   *155*
Bad Fridays and "Good Friday"   *159*
Go Tell John   *163*
"What Doesn't Destroy Me Makes Me Strong"   *167*
The One Who Holds the Knife   *171*
"It Seemed Good in Thy Sight"   *175*
Don't Go through It Alone   *177*
The Pain God Bears   *181*
The Man in the Iron Mask   *185*
The Beliefs of Unbelief   *189*
Tractor-Driving, Cow-Scratching John   *191*
"Sent to Me By Heaven"   *193*

CHAPTER SEVEN

THE GOD WHO MADE YOKES

Not What They Expected   *197*
The Glory of the Ordinary   *201*
The Sacredness of the Secular   *205*
Stolen Joy   *209*

CHAPTER EIGHT

THE GOD WHO CALLS DISCIPLES

Called to Copy God *215*

Called to Maturity *217*

Called to Confess *221*

Called to Treat Transgressors Tenderly *225*

Called to Compassion *229*

Called to Befriend Sinners *231*

Called to Respect Repentance *235*

Called to Carry the Weak *241*

Called to Serve *245*

Called to Deny Self *249*

Notes *253*

Contents

◆

x

Introduction

Said God to Moses, "I am pleased with you, and I know you by name." Warmed and emboldened by this incredible kindness, the man said to God, "Now show me your glory." This sovereign Lord said he would, but there was only so much that would or *could* be seen by humans—"My face cannot . . . must not . . . be seen."[1]

For all the intimacy, for all the mercies shown to Moses and to the rebellious people, for all the willingness of God to make himself known, humans are too impure, too limited, to handle a full frontal view of God.

I think I'm reminding you of all this so you won't expect too much from this little book. Maybe I'm wanting

1

to make the point, too, that we must retain some modesty and humility when we talk about God. Colin Morris, put it like this:

> There *are* preachers who chat about God with a folksy familiarity that is breathtaking. They would be modest enough to confess they haven't the foggiest idea what is going on in the head of their family pet but lay claim to sure knowledge of what their Pal Up There is thinking about the National Economy, the Middle East conflict or even the future of Mankind.[2]

There's more to the mind, character, and purposes of God than we can scribble in the margins of our Bible, cram into our filing cabinets, or store on our hard disks.

While modesty's an essential, surely it's right for our reach to be greater than our grasp. I'm weary of reading froth and eating bubbles.

Because it was what he wanted, the Witch Queen gave Edmund Turkish Delight to eat, says C. S. Lewis.[3] But though he shoveled it into his mouth and although it tasted delightful, he always felt hungry and wanted more. Always edible, always delightful, but never satisfying.

Certain kinds of literature (and preaching) can be like that. P. T. Forsyth passionately dismissed that sort, saying, "The non-theological Christ is popular, he wins votes; but he is not mighty [to save]."[4]

Following the lead of countless others, I'm one of those who thinks that to make sense of life and to live it to the full, we must begin at God.

Discipleship is living in the image of God in whatever life situation we find ourselves. Our submission to God as followers depends on our view of him; and though we can't completely succeed in seeing him, we must pursue not our view of God but God's view of himself.

God's view of himself is Jesus Christ. "Jesus" is the human name of God; he is God, says Howard Butt, "with name, rank and serial number; God with a Galilean accent."[5] Jesus is God speaking to us in the only language we can understand, a human language spoken in a human life. Jesus is the human life of God. He is God become intimate—"God the Vague" become "God the Vital," God the faceless taking on a face.

Harry E. Fosdick wouldn't have accepted all that is claimed for Jesus Christ in these studies, but he imagines the growing convictions of the disciples concerning Jesus like this:

> At first they may have said, God sent him. After a while that sounded too cold, as though God were a bow and Jesus the arrow. That would not do. God did more than send him. So I suspect they went on to say, God is with him. That went deeper. Yet, as their experience with him progressed, it was not adequate. God was more than with him. So at last we catch the reverent accents of a new conviction, God came in him.[6]

It's correct to say that Jesus not only lived *for* God, he lived *as* God.

In these "glimpses into the life of God," I'm taking the view that the only true God has a history that shows itself in the biblical Story and culminates in his coming in the person we know as Jesus of Nazareth. It's that Story that must shape our existence and life as God's covenant community and as God's disciples.

THE GOD

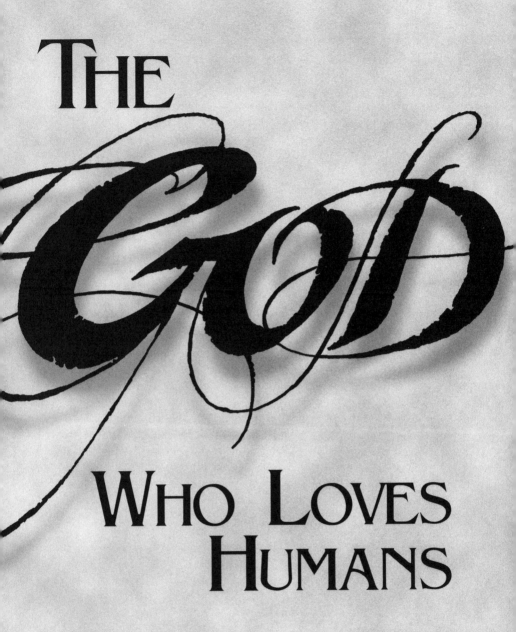

WHO LOVES HUMANS

• O N E •

"They stripped him and put a scarlet robe on him, and then twisted together a crown of thorns and set it on his head. They put a staff in his right hand and knelt in front of him and mocked him."

—Matthew 27:28

✦

A Vulnerable God

The lengths to which this God will go to express his love for us are almost beyond belief—almost, but not quite!

Sometimes God manifests himself in powerful—even frightening—ways. When Isaiah saw him, he gasped in terror and astonishment, "Woe to me! I am ruined!"[1] And when the apostles saw Jesus rebuke the wind, they recoiled in awe at this one who commanded raging storms and boiling seas to obey him.

But when Thomas saw Jesus that day in the upper room, there were no heavenly seraphim, no smoke-filled temple, no shaking of the ground. There was no threatening sea or raging storm—only a young man standing quietly in front of Thomas . . . a wounded young man . . . a lethally wounded young man. The wounds were still visible—even accessible, if Thomas had wished.

Here was someone who bore the marks of defeat. Standing in front of Thomas was a vulnerable one, one who had been beaten and put down like an unwanted dog. The staggering confession that fell from his lips was more than, "You're alive after all!" It was more than, "You're the Messiah and my Lord!" More than, "Now I believe!"

I'm dragging this out because I missed the depths of it for so long. I'm far from fully grasping it now, but much of what I missed is there to be seen and ought to be seen, needs and *begs* to be seen.

The lengths to which this God will go to express his love for us are almost beyond belief—almost, but not quite!

It isn't just that Thomas identified Jesus as God—which in itself is a profound and precious mystery—it's the *kind of God* that stood before Thomas that baffles the mind. A God who tears mountain ranges to shreds, who rolls out light years of space like a man laying carpet, a God who flings galaxies into the empty space and lays oceans in their places with an eyedropper—that kind of God, we think, earns the name "God." But a God who will be bundled into a crowded room, with spittle falling from his beard and red welts marking his face? A God like that? A God who stands silent before an insolent and pathetic little Roman governor, a God who listens patiently to the rantings of an ecclesiastical hypocrite? A God like that? A God who blushes as he is stripped naked for crucifixion, who winces as spikes gouge their way into his feet and hands? A God who delivers himself into the hands of stupid, self-serving, brutal men—*this* is the God who stood before Thomas!

But how could they have done this? Where did they get the power to kill God? How did they get within reach of him? Don't you remember what Jesus said to Pilate when the governor claimed to have the power to kill or release him? "You would have no power over me if it were not given you from above."

God made himself vulnerable. It could have happened no other way.

And why did he do it? For love of us!

> God loves to be longed for, He longs to be sought,
> For He sought us Himself with such longing and
>   love,
> He died for desire of us, marvellous thought!
> And he yearns for us now to be with Him above.[2]

This is the only true and living God!

> *"The Lord did not set his affection on you and choose you because you were more numerous than other peoples, for you were the fewest of all peoples. But it was because the Lord loved you."*
>
> —Deuteronomy 7:7

✦

Why Would He Bother?

The Christian faith says God died for love of us!

"But," you say, "God can't die!"

This is true—but he went ahead and died anyway, didn't he? He who was God became human and dwelled among us and humbled himself to death, even death on a cross.[1] I must confess that the most perplexing part of my faith is the truth that God can be bothered with us.

Have you noticed that the New Testament doesn't dwell on the gory details of the actual dying of the Lord? We're inclined to do that, to milk it for all the emotional value we can get from it. We describe the horrors of a long, slow, pain-filled, agonizing death, forgetting that

Jesus died so quickly it surprised Pilate. No, the wonder of it all was not the amount of *pain* but the amount of *love*. The power of this death was not in the *physical pain* that accompanied it but in the *holy devotion* to the will of God that motivated it. The inexpressible importance of it lay not in its *physical endurance* but in its *atoning*.

Though I read it more than thirty years ago, I'll never forget my emotional response to something E. S. Jones, a missionary to India, said. "If there were a cosmic newspaper announcing: GOD THE CREATOR OF THE UNIVERSE GIVES HIMSELF TO REDEEM A PLANET CALLED EARTH!—the universe would gasp in astonishment."[2] I did. Suddenly Jones had made me see what it was I had been paying lip service to. I had already known, if not said, such a thing, and yet . . . I had never *really* known.

Why is it so hard for me to understand *such* a love by *such* a God? Perhaps it's because I'm weary of watching a world filled with vile human beings. And perhaps it isn't just the cruel and brutal and callous people who make me sick—maybe it's the *pathetic*. Those of us who aren't viciously brutal are *banal*. We fritter away our lives with trivial pursuits, paltry causes, with the superficial, the trite, the oohing and aahing over the commonplace.

There are times when I wonder why *anyone* would bother with me, much less God.

Why would he bother?

But more than all this, I have a hard time comprehending his love because I'm weary of looking at me. Reflecting on all the loving friendship, energy, time, prayers, compassion, challenge, and teaching that has been expended on me, there are times when I wonder why *anyone* would bother with me, much less God. I think of the words of R. L. Stevenson to his father, "I hope I will one day amount to someone worth talking about, if for no other reason than you won't have wasted all your suffering on me."[3] His saying this to his father touches and moves me; my saying it to my family and friends makes sense; but God is God, and somehow that puts him out of my emotional reach.

Why would he bother with me? With you?

Putting all this together and adding to it the unutterable splendor and majesty of God, why wouldn't his love of us, his dying for us, be difficult to swallow?

But he *does* love us; he *did* die for us. That's the central affirmation of the blessed Story. And rather than believe it is too good to be true, we choose to believe it is too good *not* to be true.

Why would he die for us? Because he is God the holy Lover.

> I think this is the authentic sign and seal
> Of Godship, that it ever waxes glad.
> And more glad, until gladness blossoms, bursts
> Into a rage to suffer for mankind.[4]

Why would he do it? For love of us! And if we try to go beyond *love* in this matter, we find ourselves blocked, for in the world of the ethical, love is an ultimate; it is its own defense and explanation. End of search!

> *"Give thanks to the Lord, for he is good.*
> *His love endures forever."*
>
> —Psalm 136:1

✦

God's Loving Purpose

If you say the word "creation" to many people today, you invite a discussion about "big bangs" and evolution. But more and more scientists are joining the famed astronomer, Fred Hoyle, in saying, "Human life can't be a chance product." He went on to say that scientists who insist on a chance evolution of humans "believe in magic."[1] Mathematicians at the 1965 Wistar convention in Philadelphia said, "It's a mathematical impossibility for human life to have simply 'happened' according to known biological laws. The odds against it are so great that our computers couldn't compute them."

Yet, in spite of the evidence, many continue to hold to the desperate picture of a "universe in ruins." The famous

British philosopher, Bertrand Russell, speaking about man, said that

> his origin, his growth, his hopes and fears, his loves and his beliefs are but the outcome of accidental collocations of atoms; that no fire, no heroism, no intensity of thought and feeling, can persevere an individual life beyond the grave; that all the labors of the ages, all the devotion, all the inspiration, all the noon-day brightness of human genius, are destined to extinction in the vast death of the solar system, and that the whole temple of Man's achievement must inevitably be buried beneath the debris of a universe in ruins. . . . Only within the scaffolding of these truths, only on the firm foundation of unyielding despair, can the soul's habitation henceforth be safely built.[2]

Contrary to Russell's "unyielding despair," the Hebrew-Christian Scriptures bring us the message of a God who acted out of purposeful love, creating us and entering into a relationship with us.

Psalm 136 puts creation and redemption in one glad song with the recurring phrase, "his love endures forever." Questions are answered with this resounding proclamation:

"Why did God create the heavens?"
His love endures forever.
"Why should we say God is good and thank him?"
His love endures forever.
"Why did he place the sun and moon?"
His love endures forever.
"Why did God free us from our enemies?"
His love endures forever.

Colossians 1 does the same thing.[3] Creation and redemption are linked with the love of God as it is manifested in the person of Jesus Christ. Paul, speaking of Christ, tells us that all things were created *in* him, *through* him, and *unto* him. He is the one in and through whom God sought to reconcile the world to itself and to him.

But if God has loved us and loves us still, how do we explain the harsh realities that assault our senses and minds? *Nature, human suffering, and evil all deny the love of God.* Frozen wastes, harsh deserts, malarial insects, parasitical creatures, predatory animals, storms and earthquakes, killing and maiming, terminal wards, leukemic children, birth deformities, pitiless tyrannies—these and a thousand more realities tell their own story. And it isn't one of love and redemption.

If God has loved us and loves us still, how do we explain the harsh realities that assault our senses and minds?

But not all of nature speaks of harshness. If there is harshness to explain, there is beauty to savor. If there is illness to explicate, there is health to enjoy. If there is evil, there is breath-taking goodness; if there is callousness or blind indifference, there is spellbinding love and sacrifice.

The biblical Story urges us to believe the best and to trust until the drama has run to its final conclusion. It entreats us to trust that the one who created us in love is working for our everlasting blessing. It enjoins us to recognize our own responsibility in so much of the pain and in all of the evil. It insists that we believe our best thoughts in the worst of times and not give way to the pessimism of unbelief.

The biblical Story urges us to believe the best and to trust until the drama has run to its final conclusion.

∞

The Story of creative love says that we rebelled against our Lord and disaster befell us, but that God refused to wash his hands of us and that down through the centuries he has been working his loving purpose for us—a purpose that has come fully to light in Jesus of Nazareth.

We live on the *Visited Planet!*

*"But God demonstrates his own love for us in this:
While we were still sinners, Christ died for us."*
—Romans 5:8

✦

Cherishing the Mystery

Martin Dalby, head of music for the BBC in Scotland, said, "Bad religion answers the unanswerable; good religion cherishes the mystery."[1] Joseph Parker, the famous London preacher, in a moment of modesty confessed that there was something that baffled him more than why Jesus chose Judas. "Why did he choose me?" he gasped.[2]

I suppose the bottom line is that he loves us!

In the arena of ethical response, love has the final word. It is its own justification. When we say someone does something for love of another, that is supposed to settle it. It's true that those who have a biting awareness of their shortcomings go on to mumble, "But *how* could he?" He does!

Haven't believers down the centuries shaken their heads in joyous disbelief when, unable to get to the bottom of it all, they gratefully accepted the truth of it, that mystery or not, God was willing to die for them? When we continue to sing hymns like Robert Harkness' "Why Should He Love Me So?" we aren't asking for information, we're exulting in a mysterious truth.

Love sent my Savior to die in my stead.
Why should He love me so?
Meekly to Calvary's cross he was led.
Why should He love me so?

Nails pierced His hands and His feet for my sin.
Why should He love me so?
He suffered sore my salvation to win.
Why should He love me so?

O how He agonized there in my place!
Why should He love me so?
Nothing withholding my sin to efface.
Why should He love me so?

Why should He love me so?
Why should He love me so?
Why should my Savior to Calvary go?
Why should He love me so?[3]

The mystery is deepest for those who have the clearest understanding of their sinfulness, for those who recognize the pathetic and trivial course their lives have taken down the years. When they think of how offensive their lives must have been, and even now are, to One so holy and so selfless, they can hardly believe for joy. J. H. Jowett, believed by some to be the greatest English-speaking preacher in the world, urges us to pay heed to the truth of God's love for us, for if we do:

> We shall hear that wondrous evangel that Pascal heard, and hallowed all his years: "I love thee more ardently than thou hast loved thy sin." I know how I have loved my sin. I know how I have clung to it. I know how I have yearned after it. I know what illicit pleasure I have found in it. I know how I have pursued it at any cost. And, now, in the school of Calvary, my Master takes up this, my so strenuous and overwhelming passion for sin, and contrasts it disparagingly with his passion for me: "I love thee more than thou hast loved thy sin."[4]

The mystery is deepest for those who have the clearest understanding of their sinfulness.

∞

What power there is in such a statement! That Christ sees how we have loved our sins, yearned after them, eagerly sought them, bathed and wallowed in them, powdered and painted ourselves with them, worn them as badges of honor. He sees all that! Sees how we crave and hunger for them, and still, dismissing our fever over our sins as not even approaching the depth of his longing for us, he says, *"I love thee more than thou hast loved thy sin."*

"For the Lord will not reject his people; he will never forsake his inheritance."

—Psalm 94:14

✦

Don't Give Up on Me!

Awakenings is a bittersweet and wonderful film based on actual experiences in the life and work of neurologist Oliver Sacks. In the movie, Leonard Lowe has been awakened from a catatonic "sleep" of more than thirty years. He has been treated with a medicine by a neurologist who becomes his close friend. The drug proves to be astonishingly effective. Leonard becomes normal, and to his fresh eyes, life is incredibly wonderful—more magical and wonderful than those who are used to it can imagine.

But the medicine eventually loses its effect, and Leonard twitches, shakes, and jerks his way back into a "frozen" state. At the very beginning of his descent into paralysis, Leonard will not believe it, doesn't want to believe it, denies it, reacts violently and bitterly to it. In his bitterness and fear, he lashes out at everyone, especially those who have helped him most, before he is finally forced to face the truth: he is going under; there is no medical "fix"; life is dying in him.

In a riveting and moving scene, he clings to the wire mesh of the window to keep himself upright, shaking violently. From his twisted mouth comes the garbled speech, asking the neurologist if he can stop this. The doctor says he's trying. The victim, who has just recently learned what it is to be fully alive and doesn't want to go back into his zombie state, the victim, who hates his grotesque appearance and the crumbling of his body, pleads with the doctor, "Don't give up on me!"

We've seen people like this in our own lives. People who've wrestled with evils that were destroying them. We've seen them slip and slide out of our reach and heard them, in ten thousand ways, beg us *not to give up on them.* This is what humanity, in its more lucid moments, has said to God again and again, but God has no intention of giving up on us. In Noah's day, he appointed a rainbow to say it for him, and later, he came himself in Jesus of Nazareth to prove it beyond all reasonable doubt.

Here's how 1 John 4 puts it: "And we have seen and testify that the Father has sent his Son to be the Savior of the world. . . . And so we know and rely on the love God has for us."[1] We *know* and *trust* (rely on) the love God has for us. This is a great word, not only for Christians, but for the whole world.

He won't *ever* give up on us!

"The Son of Man did not come to be served, but to serve, and
to give his life as a ransom for many."
—Matthew 20:28

✦

This God Came to Die!

"I didn't come to be ministered to," said the Christ, "I came to minister and to give my life a ransom for many."[1] *I came to give my life!* The famous painting *The Shadow of Death,* by the nineteenth-century artist William Holman Hunt, depicts the young carpenter inside the doorway of the carpenter's shop. We see him stretching in the morning sun as his frightened mother stares at an ominous shadow falling on the wall behind him—the shadow of someone with arms outstretched, as though on a cross. It was his chosen destiny!

Imagine angels watching while God forms the earth.

"And what's that place you're making now?" they might ask.

"One day they'll call it Judea."

"And what will go there, in that mountainous area?"

"There they'll build a city called Jerusalem."

"And that little hill you're shaping just now, the one just outside this Jerusalem? Is there anything special about that?"

"That," he would say with profound, solemn joy, "that will be called Golgotha, one day, and that's where the Sovereign Lord will die to save the human race from their sin!"

And they would all descend into amazed silence.

The very creation incurred great cost to God, for even then he knew he was building the hill on which he would surrender himself in the one we know as Jesus of Nazareth.

From eternity, he was always traveling toward death.

> **Even at creation God knew he was building the hill on which he would surrender himself in the one we know as Jesus of Nazareth.**

In 490 B.C. as Xerxes was advancing into Greece, he came to Thermopylae, a small pass in central Greece. Herodotus tells us that by the time he got there, he had something like six million troops on land and sea. Gathered there to stop the advance of the powerful Persian

monarch was a mere handful of Greeks headed up by three hundred Spartans led by the Spartan king Leonidas.

When Persian troops came to check the pass, they saw three hundred warriors brushing their long hair and doing calisthenics and other such things. Back they went to their master to report that some fools with weapons were playing games in the ravine. Demaratus, a Greek physician and counselor to the Persian court, assured the king they weren't playing games—they were performing a death ritual.

These men had come to die!

Many an unmarried man had volunteered, but Leonidas insisted on taking with him men who had living sons. They never meant to come back!

Love of Sparta motivated these men—love of humanity moved this God of ours. *This God came to earth to die!* In doing this, God was commending his love toward us:

> This is how God showed his love among us: He sent his one and only Son into the world that we might live through him.[2]

> We know what love is by this, that he laid down his life for us.[3]

This God came to die!

> *"I pray that you, being rooted and established in love, may have power . . . to grasp how wide and long and high and deep is the love of Christ."*
> —Ephesians 3:17–18

✦

Love in Four Dimensions

People who are serious about the love of God in Christ will tell you that they only speak about his love to keep from saying nothing. They freely admit they don't know very much about it and that Paul was right when he said the love of Christ "surpasses knowledge."[1] It goes beyond our knowing but not beyond our sense of how precious it is.

Karl Barth is regarded by every man and his mother as the greatest theologian of the twentieth century (others will go further than that), but when they asked him what his greatest and most satisfying biblical discovery was, he said, "Jesus loves me this I know, for the Bible tells me so."

In his prayer for the Ephesian disciples, Paul asked God to root them in love so that together with all the saints they could "grasp how *wide* and *long* and *high* and *deep* is the love of Christ."[2]

God's love is wide—wide enough to embrace all humanity. Not just our little religious group, our little race, our little color, our little social stratum, our little gender, or our little nation. Ah, no, God so loved "the *world*" that he gave his Son.[3]

A college professor, offended by such a truth, said a God like that would be "an amoral loving machine." Poor ignorant little man. He doesn't seem to know that the people he is repulsed by have the potential to become people he would admire. How? you say. Our God sacrifices his way into their hearts and then *transforms* them by his love.

God's love is long. Is there any length to which it will not go? Is there any price it will not pay?

It's one thing to like, to enjoy, and to be pleased with a person. It's quite another to *love*. It's one thing to feel shallow affection, admiration, even respect for a person, but it is something more to *love*.

W. M. Clow says, "Love is not love which will not die or make the sacrifices which are sometimes more cruel than death."[4] Maybe we think that's asking too much of humans. Perhaps. But it isn't asking too much of God. And if he didn't spare his own Son but delivered him up for us all, "how will he not also, along with him, graciously give us all things?"[5]

God's love is high. The love of God tirelessly calls us *up!* The entrance of the love of God into our lives will not dishonor or cheapen us. We never live so purely, so cleanly or bravely as we live when the love of God is poured out in our hearts by the Holy Spirit.[6]

And it is a *Holy* Spirit that God gives to us. So when someone told the Galatian Christians they could live a life of wickedness since they had been freed from the law by the Spirit, Paul hotly denounced it. If someone lives in the Spirit, he told them, you will see fruit befitting the Spirit; if you see dishonorable fruit, you can be sure that person is walking after the flesh.[7]

C. S. Lewis was correct. We may love people in spite of their uncleanness, foulness, and dishonor, but we could not love them *because* of these things.[8] Because we love them (or they us), we would have to work for their cleansing, their transformation. A holy love would have to call them *up*. So it isn't at all surprising to learn that God's love seeks our honor.

God's love is deep. To love the lovable—even we find that possible. But if people begin to make demands of us, begin to get in our way or outstrip us, to say nothing of opposing us, then the veneer begins to peel away.

"Come drink from my love pool," we urge those around us when we're feeling on top of our spiritual form. But let them take us seriously, let them begin to help themselves, one drink after another, and our mood changes.

"I love you brother . . . I love you sister." But let them neglect us or dare to disagree with us, let them line themselves up with others against our cherished opinions or pet projects, and the fences go up around the pool.

But God has descended to the cesspools of this world and into the barren and cold corridors of religion to love people into life and transformation. No criminal is too far down, no slave of perversion too far gone, no evil too slimy or brutal, no person so contaminated that God will not reach out a loving hand to rescue and bless.

On a wintry day on a windswept beach, a crowd of people stood peering into the seething water. The cry had gone up, "Lost boy!" They shielded their eyes against the whipping wind and moaned in despair. Then through the ranks of the helpless and fear-filled people ran one who caught a glimpse of the dying child. He tore off his clothing as he headed out into the boiling sea in an attempt to bring the boy home.

And out in the darkness of a vast universe the cry went up, "Lost planet!" And from the battlements of heaven came the Prince himself to save the lonely little planet that was spinning its way deeper and deeper into the darkness. "Poor little planet," he said, stripping off his glory as he came.

> "Poor little planet," he said, stripping off his glory as he came.

Paul believed that if we had some real understanding of how God has loved us in Christ that it would *do* things to us: he believed we would be filled with all the fullness of God and that, in loving God back, we would be carried away with his purposes—as Paul himself had been. When Paul caught sight of the love of God, he went off like a man possessed, running throughout the world, spreading the news at awful cost. When friendly hands tried to calm him down, when they urged him to take it easy, he shrugged them off and said "the love of Christ compels me."[9]

✦

A Love That Will Not
Let Me Go

Once in a while, we get so tired we'd like to lie down,
go to sleep, and sleep for a million years—or longer.
Sometimes we're so tired of the struggle for a better life—
tired of the "losing" struggle for a better life—that we'd
like to call it a day. We'd like to let the bitterness pour out
without restraint, unbridling the anger and scorching the
earth and everyone in it. Or perhaps we'd just like to let
our passions have their way and go with the current. Ah,
the bliss of movement without struggle, drifting without
trying . . . the delicious experience of doing what comes
easily, the relaxing of tense muscles, the absence of agonizing inner wrestling and arguing—"don't debate it; just
do it!" The thought of going on with more years of spiritual

warfare just wears us out, and we almost understand the spirit of Algernon Charles Swinburne, the pessimist and decadent:

> From too much love of living,
>   From hope and fear set free,
> We thank with brief thanksgiving
>   Whatever gods may be
> That no life lives for ever;
> That dead men rise up never;
> That even the weariest river
>   Winds somewhere safe to the sea.[1]

"It isn't," the weary man said to me, "It isn't that progress requires so much energy—it's that I just don't see any progress! I'm no better, no kinder. I'm not more patient. It seems the only thing I get is more strung out! I'm tired, and I don't want to try any more. I want to drift for a while." Words like these can only come from a person who's serious about his inner life, someone for whom nobility of character matters.

People who've been looked at by Christ are never free again to live the way their poor, tired hearts sometimes wish they could.

People who've been looked at by Christ are never free again to live the way their poor, tired hearts sometimes wish they could. He loves us too much to ask less of us than he does, and in ten thousand ways he pursues us with "a love that will not let us go."

God's love for us is not sugary sweet. He will not allow us to forever "lay our heads upon his breast." His love for us is not just a *feeling*—it is an attitude and a bias toward us that will lead to different emotions depending on the circumstances and our needs.

In Dickens' *A Tale of Two Cities,* the decadent Sydney Carton says to Lucie:

> In my degradation I have not been so degraded but that the sight of you with your father, and of this home made such a home by you, has stirred old shadows that I thought had died out of me. Since I knew you, I have been troubled by a remorse that I thought would never reproach me again and have heard whispers from old voices impelling me upward, that I thought were silent for ever. I have had unformed ideas of striving afresh, beginning anew, shaking off sloth and sensuality, and fighting out the abandoned fight.[2]

Mary Webb said this of a human love that came and was lost but left the lover inconsolable and forever discontent:

> Why did you come with your enkindled eyes
> And mountain-look, across my lower way,
> And take the vague dishonour from my day
> And luring me from paltry things, to rise
> And stand beside you, waiting wistfully
> The looming of a larger destiny?
>
> Why did you with strong fingers fling aside
> The gates of possibility, and say
> With a vital voice the words I dream today?
> Before, I was not much unsatisfied;
> But since a god has touched me and departed,
> I run through every temple, broken-hearted.[3]

The plain-speaking dean of St. Paul's in London, Dean Inge, said to the man who glibly asked him, "Have you found peace since you found Christ?" "No," snapped the old man, "I found war!"

"Do not suppose that I have come to bring peace to the earth," said the Christ. "I did not come to bring peace, but a sword."[4]

God loves us too much to allow us to live like pigs! And in our better moments we're glad he does; and we know, know it in our bones, that one day we'll be thrilled beyond words that God brought "trouble" into our lives. We'll see the change—the glad, wonderful, glorious change—he has worked in us, and if someone should ask if it has been worth all the trouble, we'll say, "What trouble?"

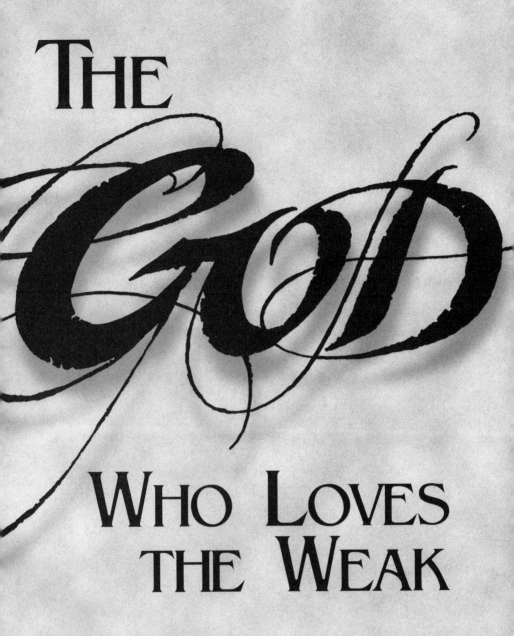

THE God

WHO LOVES THE WEAK

• TWO •

"You see, at just the right time, when we were still powerless,
Christ died for the ungodly."

—Romans 5:6

◆

Allowances

How does God view the weak? He loves them and gave
his Son to die for them.[1]

How does he view weakness—moral and spiritual
weakness, I mean? He tolerates it. He labors to free us
from weakness and bring us to maturity,[2] but he doesn't
view weakness as intolerable.

How does God view the weak? The answer to this
question is important, because it determines how God
feels toward us *all*. It is true to say that some are "weak"
and others "strong," but it is also true to say that we are
all weak. If God is against the weak, he is against us all.

God doesn't extol weakness, but he does allow it—he
makes allowances for it. He takes into account the

background, heritage, environment, and limitations of people. His Servant knows their weak frame and is merciful. He seeks to bring the weak into strength, but he adores them while they're weak. He challenges them to better and higher things, but he understands when they show vulnerability. William Lyon Phelps was once asked about the nature of friendship. He replied:

What is friendship? Alas, I am able to give you an example. A number of years ago a very intimate friend of my college days, whom everyone had regarded as a perfect example of integrity, was accused in the newspapers of a crime. I could not believe it. I was so certain of his virtue that I wrote him a letter in which I said that I and all his friends were certain that he had not done anything wrong, that he had been slandered, and that he must not feel too bad about the attack, because as long as he had the inner certainty that he had done nothing wrong, he could remain calm and serene. I received a very affectionate letter in return, and then a few days later he committed suicide. Of course I can't be certain whether I was in any way responsible for this tragedy; but what I am certain of is that I wrote him a very bad letter and that I was untrue in friendship.

Some years after this I was the subject of an attack because a press dispatch quoted me as having said something I really had not said. I received a letter from one of my former pupils. This is what he wrote to me: "I do not believe the report of your remarks is true. I do not see how you could have said that; but I want you to know that even if you did say it, my friendship and affection for you will always remain the same." That is a good letter. That is friendship.[3]

Good for the former pupil! He made it clear to Phelps that he expected lovely things of him, but he refused to put Phelps in a moral straightjacket. He expected lovely things and called Phelps to lovely things, but he allowed for failure! He learned this spirit from Jesus Christ.

Words like "weak" and "weakness" occur about eighty-seven times in the New Testament. Eighteen of them are of interest to us. Listen, there is not a word of condemnation in a single mention of weakness. There is no extolling of weakness, and there is no promoting of it; but there isn't a word of condemnation connected with it. People who say they will not grow aren't weak, they're rebels! "Weak" (in our discussion) doesn't mean impenitent or callously wicked. It means without strength, infirm. And God is *for* the weak. He even makes some people strong that they might bear the infirmities of the weak.[4]

God doesn't extol weakness, but he does allow it—he makes allowances for it.

Our God doesn't patronize the weak. And he doesn't just keep them around only as long as they show potential for becoming strong. Our God has made a total commitment to the weak in their weakness. His mind is made up! Even if they never become strong—he's going to the Cross for them! He believes in them and commits himself to them—forever!

"But you, O God, do see trouble and grief; you consider it to take it in hand. The victim commits himself to you; you are the helper of the fatherless."

—Psalm 10:14

✦

Sticking Up for the Underbird

We had just finished a lovely meal, and the conversation turned to the garden, the trees, and the bird feeders. Our gracious host confessed with some hesitancy that she worked at chasing off the sparrows and encouraging the other birds to feed. "I just don't like sparrows," she said slowly, "they're dull and plain, and I'd rather not have them around."

I have no judgment to render on that disposition, especially since I have similar feelings about certain kinds of people—on a social level, I mean. Besides, I'm not theologian enough to know if preferring jays, bluebirds, and cardinals over sparrows is an issue on which a judgment needs to be made.

But I recall Jesus assuring humans that if God cared for sparrows, which were sold for so little, he cares for humans who were of more value than sparrows. I find that comforting.

I find it even more comforting that he feels that way about *all* humans. He always seemed to be defending the wrong kind of people. Take a quick glance through the Gospels and see for yourself that he was forever speaking on behalf of the "bad" people and against the "good" people.

But surely, he was defending the *good* "bad" people against the *bad* "good" people? That's true, but it isn't the whole truth, for many of the people he defended weren't *good* "bad" people, but were openly unjust and wicked.

When people insisted on loving only the good, Jesus opposed them. "Here, look at this," we can imagine him saying, "watch how the sun shines on all those fields except the one to our left. The man who owns that field is unjust and an extortioner—watch the sun skip his field." And when it doesn't skip his field, the Master would say of God, "See, he sends his rain on the just and unjust and causes his sun to shine on the evil and the good." God makes no bones about it—*he loves humans, not just good humans.*

Jesus always seemed to be defending the wrong kind of people.

This brave, wise, gracious Lord of ours saw injustice for what it was, but he also knew that humans were sinned against as well as sinners. He saw them as hated by the World Hater and as loved—everyone of them—by the God who made them, and he came to make that transparently clear. Even the unjust were being fed on and used by Satan, and God had come to rescue them from that slavery.

It's easy to claim we would be as good, as pious, and as upright as we think ourselves to be, even if we lived under the pressures the world experiences rather than in the privileged position we occupy. It's a cheap claim too. I mean, we go on and on about how we need to raise our children in godly homes and how we need to hold back the rising tide of immorality that threatens our society. But what are we worried about? Unless a good home and all that goes with it is an advantage, why worry?

We worry because we *know* that those who are raised in good homes have an advantage. If that's the case, then those raised in bad homes are at a disadvantage. We need to remember that. It's too easy to beat people and act like top dog. We need to give the underdogs a break.

Charlie Brown says to Lucy, "This birdhouse is going to be for sparrows only."

She rasps back, "For *sparrows?* Nobody builds bird-houses for sparrows, Charlie Brown."

He grandly dismisses her remark and says, *"I* do, I always stick up for the underbird."

"Here is my servant, my chosen one in whom I delight.
A bruised reed he will not break,
and a smoldering wick he will not snuff out."

—Isaiah 42:1, 3

✦

Bruised Reeds and Smoking Wicks

If you asked God what kind of person he really liked
to be around, here's how he would describe the one who
fills his soul with delight:

> Here is my servant, whom I uphold,
>   my chosen one in whom I delight;
> I will put my Spirit on him
>   and he will bring justice to the nations.
> He will not shout or cry out,
>   or raise his voice in the streets.
> A bruised reed he will not break,
>   and a smoldering wick he will not snuff out.
> In faithfulness he will bring forth justice;
>   he will not falter or be discouraged

till he establishes justice on earth.
In his law the islands will put their hope.[1]

This one upon whom God put his Spirit, this one who would establish justice on the earth and bring hope to those in distant lands, this chosen one of God was no demagogue who "raised his voice in the streets" nor was he a cruel despot who trampled the weak, the "bruised." No, this chosen one treated the weak and the failing with kindness and gentleness! This passage from Isaiah is quoted in Matthew and applied to Jesus Christ,[2] but in 2 Timothy 2 the application is to the disciples of Christ.[3] This passage describes the character of the Christ and all who are like him. He is the Servant, and those who would be like him are fellow servants. Among the many lovely qualities that make God smile is the quality of *compassionate understanding.*

The Bible speaks of many kinds of reeds; this one, *kaneh* in Hebrew, grew up to fifteen feet tall and had several uses. When cut in a prescribed way, they could be used as measuring rods; they were also used as walking staffs.[4] And when the occasion called for it . . . they could be used as mock scepters for messianic pretenders or to offer up heavy sponges filled with vinegar to some poor sufferer on a cross.

But these reeds were hollow, and even the best ones weren't worth much—they had to be leaned on with great care because they splintered rather than bent if too much was asked of them. If they were already bruised, they were regarded as useless.

In the Isaiah passage, the One who delights God and fills him with joy is one who will not despise a bruised reed. Knowing how fragile even the best ones are, knowing how pathetic they are when already bruised, he places on them a burden so light that they will not splinter. This is how the Servant treats weak and bruised people; and the wonder of it all is this: *this fills God with joy!*

Ancient Mideastern dwellings were lit by lamps made from a bowl of oil with a strip of flax in it. When the oil was almost exhausted, the flax dried out and began to be consumed and give off smoke. The natural thing to do, and the simplest, was to reach over and snuff out the irritant between finger and thumb.

Just reach over—and poof!—one more dead wick! All perfectly understandable. All perfectly human. Who could blame anyone for getting rid of a nuisance and a useless irritant?

But this Servant, whose spirit and way filled God with delight, endured the irritation. He carefully, without overwhelming the feeble wick, removed the ash that hindered and poured in new oil so that the sputtering, languoring, almost extinguished flame could burn bright and give light. Watch how he worked—not too quickly, the wick mustn't be smothered—gently blowing, expertly removing debris, prodding and fanning until finally the struggling flicker became a strong, clean flame.

How difficult it is for us to believe that God is willing to endure us.

Our Lord has worked with bruised reeds and smoking wicks from the beginning. Mary Magdalene—a bruised reed! The Demoniac of Gadara—a smoking flax! The cursing and bragging Peter, the "doubting" Thomas, the ruthless Pharisee called Saul—"bruised reeds."

What a Lord! What a Father who finds delight to the depths of his soul in such a Servant. What a Father to uphold his Servant in that kind of work. Haven't I read somewhere, "Jesus of Nazareth with the Holy Spirit and power . . . went around doing good and healing all who were under the power of the devil, because God was with him"?[5] *Because* God was with him, he went around doing these things!

But Christ isn't naive. He knew of Peter's loud mouth and his coming denials. He knew the apostolic scattering was coming when the Shepherd would be smitten. He accepted the pain that all of this would bring—and he trusted them. He trusted them before they let him down, he trusted them during the pain that their weakness brought him, and he maintained that trust until their wavering days were over and he met them at heaven's gate to welcome them home. "Well done, well done," he would have said, eyes shining with admiration. "Welcome home."

How difficult it is for us to believe that God is willing to endure us, we who are so far beneath him, we who are intimidated by his holiness and unutterable majesty. But whenever we have difficulty understanding God and his love, we can look at Jesus Christ.

Don't you remember that, just before they crucified him, they shoved a broken reed into his hand for a scepter? They were doing more than they knew. *Right there, close to his heart, they made him hold a broken reed.* It suited him; no scepter made of precious metal or studded with the world's wealth in precious stones would have symbolized his royalty so well.

> *"Now the tax collectors and 'sinners' were all gathering around to hear him. But the Pharisees and the teachers of the law muttered, 'This man welcomes sinners and eats with them.'"*
>
> —Luke 15:1–2

✦

Receiver of Wrecks

You've noticed, of course, that God, in the person of Jesus of Nazareth, was always getting into trouble with the religious, church-going people. Yes, it was the right-living, devout types he offended most. Don't you find that very interesting?

He was always defending certain people against these "good" types, and that's what created much of his difficulty. But it's *who* he was defending that really gets our attention. It seems he was forever defending the "sinners" against the "righteous," and he was often found hanging around the immoral, the outsiders, the churchless people of ill repute.

51

All this makes for great preaching and fine writing (if you can preach or write well). It rolls easily off the tongue and pen, and we church-going, righteous people are sure it's the kind of thing you *should* say about God. Hmmm.

Luke tells us they were offended at his eating with sinners and tax collectors.[1] That really got their attention; for surely, if he were a holy man, he would have hung around holy people—that's what good people are expected to do—hang around good people.

What should have gotten their attention and didn't was that the *publicans and sinners hung around Jesus!* In this there is something of a mystery. How is it that these moral wrecks and religiously sidelined people *wanted* to be around the most God-conscious man who ever lived?

What was there about him that drew sinners into his presence?

It wasn't that he was naive about their character—when he pictures them in the parable of the "Prodigal Son," he describes them as self-serving, immoral, self-dishonoring brats! It wasn't that he soft-pedaled the issue of sin. No, this young rabbi not only spoke against sin, he lived against it. And he was so enraged by it that he died to destroy it and all its fruit, so enraged by it that there was no price he wouldn't pay to rescue humans from its clutches. He despised and loathed its every form—crass or respectable, flesh or spirit, deed or disposition.

So what was there about him that drew sinners into his presence? He made them believe that God meant them no harm—that he loved them in their lostness and that he came to rescue them from it and give them the fullness of life!

Marcus Dodds tells us that when God sat in village streets watching the people, he thought they looked like donkeys plodding their weary way under their heavy burdens, heads down and legs dragging. He saw them as the (almost) indifferent ox that knew of nothing better, dragging its yoke from one end of the field and back, day after day, until, with its strength wasted, it was disposed of.[2]

He saw them as poor, pathetic people—lost among the stars, wandering up and down on a planet that was spinning its ways into eternal darkness. He saw them as people in need of peace and rest. He saw them as people who endured fruitless labor, without satisfaction or hope. Toiling day after day to make ends meet, they added to their burdens by chaining themselves with sinful habits, the pursuit of superficial pleasures, and sinful indifference to what God might have in mind for them. And by doing this, they burdened themselves further with fear and remorse. Giving up on themselves, they gave up on everyone else and banded together only to make the loneliness not so lonely and the time go more quickly as they traveled on to the grave.

And so God himself sent them a message, a Story, and he put it into the hands of influential leaders and teachers who were supposed to tell its loving truth, were supposed to tell it to these who saw themselves as people beyond redemption.

And what did these teachers do? Instead of bringing this joyous message to their fellow sinners, "the righteous" gorged themselves on it and shut the love of God off from anyone who didn't meet their standards of behavior and doctrine. Instead of recognizing the tired and weakened condition of these hopeless ones, they laid on them the further burden of *a joyless religion.*

It was to these tired, weak people—ancient and modern—that Jesus said, "Come to me, all you who are weary and burdened, and I will give you rest. Take my yoke upon you and learn from me, for I am gentle and humble in heart, and you will find rest for your souls. For my yoke is easy and my burden is light." [3]

♦

"He tends his flock like a shepherd: He gathers the lambs in his arms and carries them close to his heart; he gently leads those that have young."

—Isaiah 40:11

✦

The Shepherd King

The good news is this: there is only one God, and he's just like Jesus Christ! When the Good Shepherd finally made his appearance, he was as the prophet Isaiah had described him. We have this word from God to those who were to speak in his name:

> You who bring good tidings to Zion,
>   go up on a high mountain.
> You who bring good tidings to Jerusalem,
>   lift up your voice with a shout,
> lift it up, do not be afraid;
>   say to the towns of Judah,
>   "Here is your God!"

See, the Sovereign Lord comes with power,
　and his arm rules for him.
See, his reward is with him,
　and his recompense accompanies him.
He tends his flock like a shepherd:
　He gathers the lambs in his arms
and carries them close to his heart;
　he gently leads those that have young.[1]

For years, they had endured the taunt, "Where is your God?" Now those commissioned by God announced with the zeal of assurance, "Behold your God!" And when the helpless looked, they looked toward the wilderness and saw God, the sovereign Lord. This powerful Lord had exercised his power against the oppressors and had won his reward, which he was bringing with him. And what was that reward? His redeemed people, his "flock." For all his power, the Lord "gathers the lambs in his arms . . . he gently leads those that have young."

He leads gently and slowly because among the flock are rubbery-legged lambs who tire easily and need to be picked up and carried.

He leads gently and slowly because among the flock are rubbery-legged lambs who tire easily and need to be picked up and carried, and there are waddling expectant mothers and mothers with brand new babies who can't keep up very well. The sovereign power of this God doesn't blind him to the needs of the vulnerable.

Watching out for the needy and the infirm isn't just his philosophy, it's how he lived when he was here. The powerful God of Isaiah 40 is revealed to us as Jesus of Nazareth who brought out the meaning of God, who exegeted him, who made the life of God visible.

It isn't hard to imagine the strong, young bucks in the flock wanting to move faster and farther than the ewes heavy with child or the tottering new arrivals are able. "There are fresh fields ahead, new pastures, fresh water. Let's get rolling here! What's holding us up?" All this from healthy, strong sheep who have forgotten the days when they, too, were vulnerable and weak and couldn't feed or water themselves. The shepherd looked out for the good pasture and for fresh, clean water, he guided them away from danger, and he was the one who defended them against all the predators so that they now stood strong and fast and healthy.

Strong and fast and healthy and—impatient, compassionless, smug, self-righteous, forgetful, and ungrateful.

Yes, but . . .

No buts, God loves the weak and vulnerable.

✦

Where Are the Stretchers?

Ezekiel 34 delivers a scathing denunciation of the leaders of God's people.

> Woe to the shepherds of Israel who only take care of themselves! Should not shepherds take care of the flock? You eat the curds, clothe yourselves with the wool and slaughter the choice animals, but you do not take care of the flock. You have not strengthened the weak or healed the sick or bound up the injured. You have not brought back the strays or searched for the lost. You have ruled them harshly and brutally. So they were scattered because there was no shepherd, and when they were scattered they became

59

food for all the wild animals. My sheep wandered over all the mountains and on every high hill. They were scattered over the whole earth, and no one searched or looked for them.[1]

Here is God, as Joseph Parker would have it, "standing up for the masses" against the whip-cracking bosses who went under the name of "shepherds."[2]

But when did God ever do otherwise?

His red-hot criticism of the leaders was not because they hadn't filled the temple coffers or led the nation in successful wars against the heathen or because they didn't structure the worship well or defend the faith against pagan philosophies! It didn't matter to God at this point that there were no foreign kings going to Jerusalem to pay homage to him.

He wasn't asking, "Where are the hosts of converts?" but "Where are the stretchers?" What had they done for the sick? Why weren't the leaders coming in, weary but smiling, with their arm around the once lost? Why weren't the strong absent from the usual haunts because they were out attending to those who were straying? Where was the help for the wounded and injured? Who was carrying the weak and tottering?

Where were the stretchers?

Verse 4 speaks of the weak, the sick, the injured, the straying, and the lost. *These* were the people God was standing up for, and God had to do it—nobody else would! He saw no splints made for the injured, no crowds of thrilled people around the shamed prodigal; he heard no shouts of joy over wanderers led home. All that *bothered* him. He saw the weak and sick and straying go to the wall!

Doesn't that say something about the kind of humans God cares for? If he scorched the leaders for *not* attending to these matters, he is telling us in the plainest of terms what he expects of leaders in regard to this class of people.

I'm not extolling weakness, I'm making a plea for those of us who are weak. Weakness doesn't cry or blush easily, but weak people do. I'm not opposed to you who are strong; I'm just committed to us who are weak! To jettison the weak, the diseased, and the broken is not Godlike. It may be "good business sense" to cut your losses, to spend time only with the "fast horses" in the stable so you can build a strong organization—but it isn't God's way!

Mike Yaconelli wrote, "I believe evangelicals have sold their birthright for a mess of porridge. We have been seduced by the glitter and temporariness of power and have gone a whoring. We have sold out and traded our worship of God for the worship of power. We have changed the ministry of sacrifice for the ministry of domination."[3] All this shows in our willingness to cater only to the "players" while the weak perish.

I'm not opposed to you who are strong; I'm just committed to us who are weak!

Ah, but leaders often have settled views about the weak and "nonproductive." To get their work done, their very demanding work, to get it growing and glowing, they often think the weak will have to take care of themselves: "We assembled and discussed the matter, Lord, and we all voted for the survival of the fittest." And how would God feel about such a decision? Would he not say, "I was sick and naked and lonely and cold and hungry and imprisoned and broken and *weak* . . . and you voted for the survival of the fittest?" And might we not say, "Lord, when were you sick and lonely and hungry and broken and *weak* and we let you go to the wolves?" And what will we say if he should reply, "In as much as you did it unto the *least* of these *my brethren,* you did it unto me?"[4]

♦

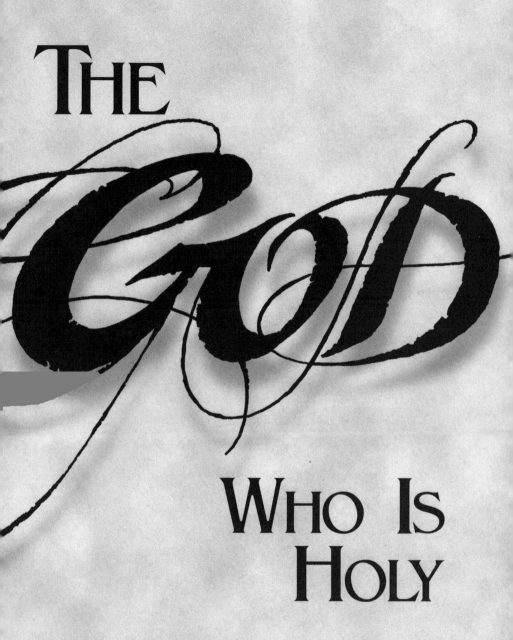

THE GOD

WHO IS HOLY

• T H R E E •

> *"God made him who had no sin to be sin for us, so that in him we might become the righteousness of God."*
>
> —2 Corinthians 5:21

✦

A Love That Can Be Trusted

A "love" that isn't holy can't be trusted, and a "love" that finds no offense in corruption and cruelty isn't holy. A "love" that yawns at my sin will yawn at the sin of others, will yawn at the sin of a planet, will yawn at the sin of a universe. A god who loves like that is no god worthy of worship. A god like that is not a righteous god; he is morally contemptible.

There's too much sweetness and light, too much of the "Heavenly Sweetheart" about a god who approaches us in our great wickedness and says, "There, there, you didn't mean to be bad." We *do* mean to be bad. And what's more, there are times when we *know* we mean to be bad, and there are times when we would be worse if we didn't fear reprisal! We're especially clear on this matter if we're on the receiving end of injustice and degeneracy.

Sinners are sometimes willing "to let bygones be bygones"; that, however, is only another mark of their sinfulness, another proof that they have no more than a vague impression of what holiness is and an even vaguer notion of what divine holiness is. But a holy God *cannot* overlook sin.

When we offend God, it isn't enough for us to offer our repentance, saying, "Let that satisfy!" The repentance of sinful people to satisfy an offense against a holy God? Our repentance doesn't even satisfy ourselves, doesn't even satisfy our fellow-sinners; why would we dare think it would satisfy a holy God?

But God *wanted* to forgive us; he *longed* to forgive us; and so he justified forgiving us by providing us a repentance that *would* suffice—the repentance of Christ. We can offer *that* in faith.

There was a *man* called Jesus Christ, whose forefathers were Abraham, David, and the prophets, whose mother was Mary, whose teacher was Moses, and whose God was Yahweh. This man so identified himself with the holiness of God that he offered him nothing less than complete, holy obedience.

This man so identified himself with his sinful fellow humans that he submitted to the call of repentance, and though free from personal sin, took upon himself the judgment due humanity's sin. He so identified himself with sinful humanity that he could and did confess our confession that "we have sinned against thy holy Self and dishonored your holy name." On the Cross he died our death, bearing our sin, confessing for us the justice of the holy judgment that now concentrates itself on him who has come to be humanity's representative.

At last! At last there was one, this Jesus of Nazareth, who knew what God's holiness meant from humanity's perspective and who knew what human sin was from God's perspective. Finally there was one in whom the holiness of God and the sinfulness of humans could meet and be demonstrated—not just illustrated—but demonstrated in an actual life within the sinful human family.

The Cross of Christ is the one place in time and space where we see beyond all dispute that *holy* love *can* be trusted. In the life and death of Jesus Christ, the holiness of God is brought home to us, a holiness so holy that God must justify himself—in the eyes of sinners, no less—for extending forgiveness.

Forgiveness without divine holiness is forgiveness without moral basis.

Forgiveness without divine holiness is forgiveness without moral basis. There would be no righteousness, no justice, no holiness in such a forgiveness.[1] But God's forgiveness is founded in his holy abhorrence of sin and the all-sufficient sacrifice of Christ. And all of this because God, the holy Lover, would have it so! This is a love that can be trusted!

> *"Who among the gods is like you, O Lord? Who is like you—*
> *majestic in holiness, awesome in glory, working wonders?"*
> —Exodus 15:11

✦

God's Ethical Holiness

The ancient gods of India were celebrated in the kinds of bawdy songs they sing in bars and brothels; the Phoenician gods were personified cruelty and lust; the Canaanite deities were faithless liars; the Greek gods were decadent, drunken, brutal, incestuous, vindictive, and murderous clods. The pagan heavens were peopled with immoral thugs who practiced with glee every piece of vile trash imaginable. And then along came Moses, and speaking for a God who called himself YHWH, he said: "Be holy; for I am holy!"[1]

Biblically, holiness carries with it the common ancient idea of separateness, difference, not the same, other than!

That certainly would cover the nature of the God who revealed himself to Israel as YHWH. But that wasn't nearly enough. Different in what way? One orange, while it is like another orange, is still a different orange, not the same, and other than all other oranges.

So how was Yahweh different? While the other gods were based on fanciful myths, this God was the creator and sustainer of the universe and all in it. And this God—the creator of light, harmony, fruitfulness, and life—showed his unsurpassed power in the days of Moses by "uncreating" Egypt. He rebuked the light and made darkness, he took harmony and produced chaos, he took fruitfulness and cursed it with barrenness, and he made the waters teem with death rather than life. The creator produced uncreation and brought curses on those who cursed his people and exposed their gods as less than nothing. Moses and Israel put it like this: "Who among the gods is like you, O Lord? Who is like you—majestic in holiness, awesome in glory, working wonders?"[2]

But it was more than Yahweh's power, majesty, and creative ability that made him different from the mythical beings worshiped by others. His holiness had an *ethical quality,* a *righteousness,* about it. And because this God was righteous and pure and couldn't condone what was wicked,[3] he called Israel to a life of holiness.[4] This call outlined a lifestyle that embraced loyalty, generosity, pity, honesty, truthfulness, righteousness, love, and sexual purity, as well as devotion to Yahweh alone.

David simply and grandly says that God "is good and upright," and that's why he teaches sinners his ways and guides the humble in what is right.[5] Psalm 24 makes the connection between holiness and how life should be lived if people want to be acceptable in the presence of Yahweh.

Who may ascend the Eternal's hill?
    Who may stand within his sacred shrine?
He only who has clean hands and a heart
    unstained,
    Who never sets his mind on what is false,
        who never breaks his word;
Such are the men who are in quest of him,
    who seek the presence of the God
    of Jacob.[6]

Can you imagine what a horror it would be to have a God who was not holy, who was not opposed to unrighteousness and uncleanness? Now that he has taught us and shown us what goodness is, wouldn't it be horrific beyond speech to discover he cared nothing for kindness, compassion, uprightness, purity, generosity, and justice? But this is an ethical God who can be depended on to make righteous judgments.[7]

Both Testaments assure us of his righteousness and justice. Don't we hear the psalmist say the whole world should rejoice at the thought of a God who cares about a glad-hearted justice?

Say among the nations, "The Lord reigns."
    The world is firmly established, it cannot
        be moved;
    he will judge the peoples with equity.
Let the heavens rejoice, let the earth be glad;
    let the sea resound, and all that is in it;
    let the fields be jubilant, and everything
        in them.
Then all the trees of the forest will sing for joy;
    they will sing before the Lord, for he
        comes,
    he comes to judge the earth.

He will judge the world in righteousness
and the peoples in his truth.[8]

And when the New Testament speaks of God forgiving our sins, it speaks of a forgiveness that is not only "faithful" but "righteous."[9] There is nothing *immoral* about the forgiveness we receive through the atoning death of Christ. A loving God promises forgiveness and keeps his word—he is faithful. And there is nothing *dishonorable* about that forgiveness, for sin is not treated lightly; it is not seen as trivial. And nothing about this forgiveness will *undermine* holiness or suggest a weak-kneed indulgence of what is corrupt and evil. It is a forgiveness that *promotes* holiness and righteousness.

God vindicates his right to forgive sin by bringing it to us through the death of Jesus Christ.

God vindicates his right to forgive sin by bringing it to us through the death of Jesus Christ.[10] The Christ who was delivered up "for our transgressions" was delivered up because God wouldn't spare even him.[11] Rather than weakening the biblical witness to God's holiness, the Cross underscores it. Were it not for his love, there would have been no Cross. But if his love were not holy, there would have been no need for the Cross.

"For God did not call us to be impure, but to live a holy life."
—1 Thessalonians 4:7

✦

More Than Pardon

If all God offers us is pardon, he offers only half a gospel. We want more than pardon; we want *deliverance* —we want spiritual healing, moral health. It is one thing to receive divine pardon; it's another to be delivered from the power of evil ways and wicked choices.

It's because God is himself holy that we can be sure we will gain holiness. It's because he cannot and will not tolerate the presence of sin that we can know he will work to destroy it in us. The hunger we feel to be and think and behave righteously is the work of God in us. Will he who creates the hunger not fill us?[1]

What pathetic people we'd be if we craved pardon but wanted to go on wallowing in sin. If such people did procure pardon from God, they would have no life with him, no relationship with him. It's impossible to have life and relationship with God if what I want is immunity with a license to sin! And if the unthinkable were possible—if we could have fullness of life with a god who gives us a complete license to sin, that god would be our worst nightmare.

For God to bring us out of the darkness of our deep prison into the sunlight only to leave us permanently fettered with the chains of the wickedness that thrust us down into that prison in the first place—that would be to bring us less than we need. It would be to bring less than *he* could be satisfied with. For God to bring us to the point of repentance, to create within us a healthy hatred of all that is unlike him and yet to tell us there is no power on earth or in heaven by which we can be changed—that would be a message of despair. To pardon us and allow us to live in his presence without giving us the heart that would adore his presence, respect his holy character, will his will, and rejoice in his majesty—that would leave us crippled. We'd be in sight of the shore but permanently adrift.

And if it is holiness we want, God will go after it in us and will not ask us if we're happy about the way he pursues it.

It is nothing less than *life* in relationship with himself that God offers us. That friendship, that unbroken fellowship of love must have holiness at its heart because he who called us is holy. And because he is holy, only that which is holy can survive his completed work in us. All else is doomed to destruction.

Because he is the source of life, we find life in him; and because he is the source and embodiment of holiness, we can be sure that we will be made holy. First Thessalonians 5 gives us this assurance:

> May God himself, the God of peace, sanctify you through and through. May your whole spirit, soul and body be kept blameless at the coming of our Lord Jesus Christ. The one who calls you is faithful and he will do it.[2]

He will not settle for less, and if our will is to will and do his will, our perfected holiness is assured because the one who calls us is faithful, "and he will do it."

But there is one thing we need to be clear about—it must be holiness we want and not mere pardon; it must be holiness we want and not merely the sugary sweet "love" we hear so much of. And if it is holiness we want, God will go after it in us and will not ask us if we're happy about the way he pursues it.

✦

The Gift of Holiness

We cannot make it right. We cannot restore the disharmony we have introduced into the moral order. If we could, it would no longer be above us—we would be the fixers, the menders, the creators. Only God in Christ can bring everything back into harmony.[1]

We may sorrow and amend, but we cannot atone and reconcile. Our apologies and our sadness express our regret, but they cannot atone. Our repentance cannot atone either, for it is merely the humble fruit of godly sorrow.

There are those who strenuously insist that *justification* is the work of God for us, but deny that *holiness* is his work in us. They read the texts that call God's people to pursue holiness, to walk in holiness, or to be holy, and they conclude from them that holiness is *our* work, that it is our grateful response to God's gracious forgiveness.

The danger in this, for all its good intentions, is that it masks the freeness of salvation and life with God. It's too tempting to sinners like us to believe that we justify God's forgiving us by how well we respond to him. "I earned nothing, of course," we're willing to say, "but didn't I repent magnificently?"

If you need proof of this, you only have to see how prone we are to self-righteousness. You only have to notice how quickly we doubt others' relationships with God because they continue to struggle against sin in their lives—*as if we don't struggle in ours!*

We justify God's forgiving us by how well we respond to him. "I earned nothing, of course," we're willing to say, "but didn't I repent magnificently?"

We don't for a moment doubt our own relationship with God—despite the fact that we continue to struggle against sin—so why do we doubt theirs? It's because we see ourselves as better than others! And it's that "better than others" that gives us our "assurance." Grateful response becomes the ground of our assurance before God. Our moral achievement, *our* moral achievement, our holiness, becomes our means or our assurance of acceptance with God.

But all we are and all we have are gifts from God. We don't even *believe* on our own—we believe through grace.[2] Our *repentance,* too, is a gift of God.[3] And it is God who *works in us* to will and do his good pleasure, and it is God who fully *equips* us with everything good for doing his will and who works in us what is pleasing to him.[4]

Of course, repentance is not forced on us. Of course, it's possible to resist God's overtures toward us. But how does this change the fact that our grateful response is the work of God in us? Salvation is a gift of God that we can refuse, but when by his grace we believe and accept it, it is no less a gift—we haven't earned it.

When we make holiness *our* work, we shift the focus to our *accomplishments* and off *faith.* Our accomplishments point to us, while faith points to someone else. Isn't this, in the end, what being "justified by faith in Christ"[5] means—that we point away from ourselves when someone asks us where our salvation lies?

The constant refrain of both Testaments is that *God* makes us holy.

> This will be a sign between me and you for the generations to come, so you may know that I am the Lord, who makes you holy.[6]

> Keep my decrees and follow them. I am the Lord, who makes you holy.[7]

> Christ loved the church and gave himself up for her to make her holy.[8]

> Jesus also suffered outside the city gate to make the people holy.[9]

Only God is holy in an underived sense. All other people or things are holy because of their relationship with him. Once he has claimed them for his own, they are withdrawn from common (profane) use. They must be used—or if we're talking about people—they must engage themselves only in things that reflect God's holy will for them.

This implies that there are two senses of "holy." Persons are holy when God sets them apart for himself—that is *positional* holiness. Israel and the church were called out and sanctified by God for himself. They were different by virtue of that call and by their entering into a covenant relationship with him.[10]

Having "been sanctified"[11]—note the passive tense—God's people, then, are to *live* as those who have been sanctified. As a holy nation (and as persons within that holy nation), they were to pursue a lifestyle in keeping with their already existing status. This is *subjective* holiness.

Neither of these conditions is *forced* on God's people. The initiative in sanctification is always of God. The ongoing transformation of a willing people into the likeness of Jesus Christ is also the work of God.[12]

There is nothing in our response to God that should lead us to think we are inherently more worthy than the weakest of his disciples. Having thanked God for enriching the Corinthians, Paul assured them: "He will keep you strong to the end, so that you will be blameless on the day of our Lord Jesus Christ. God, who has called you into fellowship with his Son Jesus Christ our Lord, is faithful."[13] Having given that assurance, he went on to rebuke them for their feelings of pride and superiority, "For who makes you different from anyone else? What do you have that you did not receive? And if you did receive it, why do you boast as though you did not?"[14]

Our holiness, *positional* and *subjective,* is the work of God for us and in us—it is a *gift from God.*

"Not that I have already obtained all this, or have already been made perfect, but I press on to take hold of that for which Christ Jesus took hold of me."

—Philippians 3:12

✦

"And Maddest of All . . ."

In the musical adaption of *Don Quixote de La Mancha,* Cervantes has been thrown into prison. When his fellow prisoners learn he is a poet of the theater, they begin to make sport of him. One critic angrily rebukes the dreamer. Poets, he snarls, are mad men who spin nonsense out of nothing and take men's eyes off reality. This, he said, was a great wrong; it was a flight from the facts, and people should be made to face life as it really is, rather than dream.

Cervantes looks around at the filth and squalor of the prison and thinks of the injustice that landed them all in it. Must people settle for life as it is? Is dreaming for something better, really madness? Cervantes tells his chief critic that he has traveled the world, been enslaved, fought in war, and held his friends as they were dying.

These were men who saw life as it is but they died despairing. No glory, no brave last words only their eyes filled with confusion, questioning why! I do not think they were asking why they were dying, but why they had ever lived. Life itself seems a lunatic. Who knows where madness lies. Perhaps to be too practical is madness. To surrender dreams, this may be madness. To seek treasure where there is only trash, too much sanity may be madness. And maddest of all, to see life as it is and not as it could be, as it should be.[1]

There is an "unholy" discontent that is without thankfulness for what good there is. And because it lacks a warm gratitude, it's altogether unlike "holy" discontent— that blessed hunger that leaves us dissatisfied with things as they are. Our dreams should always exceed our grasp in what is holy. When we're healthy, there will be that pleasure in the good that already is, in the progress we've already made; but there will always be the delicious vision of what is purer, what is better and more holy.

There is a "holy" discontent that leaves us dissatisfied with things as they are.

If Abraham had wanted to go back to Mesopotamia, he could have done so. But he didn't want to; he had his eyes on another country, one that was to be given to him by God. And because that is how he felt, because he wouldn't settle for less, "God is not ashamed to be called [his] God."[2]

Isn't that a lovely thing to know? Had Abraham returned to Mesopotamia, he would have been settling for less. While, humanly speaking, that might have been understandable, wouldn't there have been a flicker of disappointment in God's eye? As it was, Abraham trusted God for the fulfillment of the promise and a glorious future. And God, beaming with pleasure, said, *"That* old man is one of my followers."

And when the days roll by and we seem no better, no holier, when the seemingly unchangeable realities of life appear to crush to silence all hope of a lovelier future, when it seems to be only madness to deny the harsh but brute facts of our spiritual lives—then we need to remember his promise that he will supply our every need according to his glorious riches in Christ Jesus.[3] Then we will recognize the surrender of our dreams—dreams that are the product of his holy promise—for the madness that it really is. And we will dig our reluctantly discarded dreams out of the trash can, dust them off, and with a smile, confess they are ours.

And God will see and will not be ashamed to be called our God.

"Jesus Christ gave himself for us to redeem us from all wickedness and to purify for himself a people that are his very own, eager to do what is good."

—Titus 2:13–14

✦

The Loving Holiness of God

Not everyone is frightened by the holiness of God. One cartoonist has a man reading a large sign on a door: *Prepare to Meet Thy God!* In the next box he shows the man straightening his tie.

Only those who haven't been drowned in the flood of egalitarianism that has engulfed the Western world still quake when they think of a holy God. The loss of awe and reverence can be seen even in worship; but for sensitive souls, the holiness of God reminds them of their sinfulness. More than that, it *reveals* to them their sinfulness. It probably isn't true that our sinfulness reveals God's holiness. It's more surely the case that God's holiness reveals our sinfulness.

85

Asked if he was afraid of God, C. S. Lewis said of course he wasn't, and yet . . . he confessed, he was. When Christ caused fish to multiply in the seas, Peter thought of the holy God who did the same in the Old Testament, and he gasped and begged Jesus, "Depart from me, for I am a sinful man, O Lord." When the prophet Isaiah saw and heard the seraphim cover their eyes in the presence of Yahweh as they tirelessly declared his holiness, he was compelled to confess his ruin and uncleanness.

Their reactions are surely healthy and to be expected as well as promoted. Just the same, it's of the utmost importance that we find balance here. *The holiness of God doesn't seek the destruction of the sinner, but the destruction of sin and the restoration of life for the sinner!*

Holy is what God *is,* and the life he offers in relationship with himself must have that character. It *cannot* be otherwise—there's nothing arbitrary about it. The life he offers is life that is lived in that spirit—a spirit of holiness. The person who has life with God is the person who confesses the nature of God as holy and who wants a relationship with the Holy One. That means holiness is esteemed, praised, and sought by those who live *with* and *in* God.

The holiness of God doesn't seek the destruction of the sinner, but the destruction of sin and the restoration of life.

And it's because God wants us to have life with him more than we want to have life with him—it's because this is true—that he sought and seeks the destruction of all that is opposed to his own holiness. But he rages against unholiness *on behalf of* the sinner he longs to live with—he rages against all unholiness within and around us; he rages against all unholiness in his own people and in those who aren't yet his.

God's holiness is not an independent quality in him— it is an aspect of his person. The last word with God is *love,* and holiness is part of that love. As "white light" may be seen to be made up of various hues, so love may be broken down into various components: holiness is one of them. There is no love that is really love that isn't holy; and there's certainly no love that is the love of God that isn't holy.

The holy God is the loving God who pursues us to make us clean and strong and pure and all the other things we associate with holiness. This holiness isn't something that has a life of its own—it's the loving God at work "cleaning us up."

He means us no harm!

THE God

WHO FORGIVES SINS

✦

Forgiveness and Repentance

Once a sinner, always a sinner! From the moment of my first sin, I can never be as though I have never sinned. From that moment on, my blessed state before God as someone forgiven is different from the blessedness of the sinless ones.

The person whose sin is not imputed to him or her is a very different being from the person who never committed sin. It was not sin that sinned—*I* sinned and changed my state before God.

But the good news begins with the word "repent." Because it is an imperative—"Repent!"—it isn't an option. There is no negotiation. But because it is an imperative, it tells us we aren't beyond redemption; by his grace, we are *able* to turn to him! God would not call a corpse to repent; he would not call to repentance what is incapable of repenting.

And because repentance is "unto the forgiveness of sins," it creates hope and gives assurance. Since he calls us to repent, it means he hasn't finished with us despite our evil, it means he continues to care, it means he wants us to be forgiven and so to turn back.

However precisely we would define the relation of repentance to forgiveness, this we know: *without repentance, there is no forgiveness!*

Repentance looks back in sorrow at where we've been and forward with eagerness to a holy life that knows full forgiveness. Repentance is a mind that by God's grace renounces the sinful past as unacceptable and purposes a future pleasing to God.

To teach that God joyfully forgives is not to teach that we should feel no sorrow.

There is no way to determine the "quantity" of sorrow that must be in repentance—that will differ from person to person, depending on our emotional makeup—but we would expect something other than a twinkling eye. Horace Bushnell spoke of "the wholly joyful" nature of repentance, but Robert Mackintosh is surely right— Bushnell's "statement is painfully jaunty. Repentance is not repentance if he dances along whistling a bright tune and asking all the world to admire him for a fine fellow." [1]

To teach that God joyfully forgives is not to teach that we should feel no sorrow. "The sacrifices of God are a broken spirit; a broken and contrite heart, O God, you will not despise."[2] To stroll into God's presence to receive forgiveness—hands in pocket, cap at a rakish angle, wearing a silly grin—is hardly the spirit the psalmist had in mind.

Those sensitive to God's holiness and their sinfulness will feel the burden of sorrow, but those, says Mackintosh, "who are in a hurry to forgive themselves, and who find the valley of humiliation unendurable, have reason to fear that they are hurrying away from God."[3]

What is true in the presence of God whom we have offended would be true also in the presence of his children whom we have offended. We mustn't breeze into the presence of those we've injured, smilingly drop our apology, and expect an automatic forgiveness. People aren't slot machines, and relationships aren't faulty carburetors.

Without repentance, there can be no forgiveness.

But repentance is not an isolated act of the mind about an isolated act of sin. It is a state of mind about all our sinful ways. When we repent of a specific sin, we turn the focus of the already existing repentant heart on that particular manifestation of our sinfulness. So it's legitimate to say we repent of specific sins, but we miss the point if we suggest that biblical repentance only exists at the moment we repent of some specific wrong.

Before we come to Christ, we have a mind about sin. When we hear his call, we adopt a new mind about sin— his! That mind, that frame of reference, becomes ours by a permanent choice. As long as we are Christ's, we live with that mind; our lives in relation to sin and holiness are shaped within that mindset. Though we sin, we never justify or whitewash it. To have a "mind" other than that of Christ's is not to be in relationship with him.

Because this is true, we don't always make a drama out of a crisis when loved ones hurt us. We don't insist on a confrontation, a conviction, a confession, an apology, and a promise of better treatment in the future from our friends or family each time some injury is done us.

Though there is no verbal or other apology for some rudeness or thoughtlessness, we judge their behavior in light of *their characteristic attitude toward and treatment of us.* We acknowledge that this behavior is unacceptable, but we also acknowledge that it is not a fair representation of their relationship to us.

There may come a time, due to the seriousness and/or frequency of the wrong—for their benefit and for ours—that we must confront them and remind them of the nature of the relationship and ask them to examine their treatment of us. Not only is this legitimate, it is a token of our love for the transgressor.[4]

"Unless you repent, you too will all perish."[5]

✦

If Our Hearts Condemn Us

To say, "I believe in the forgiveness of sins," is not the same as saying, "I believe my sins are forgiven."

"Forgiveness," said H. B. Swete, "is an act of God that may or may not be followed immediately by a sense of relief."[1]

It seems we're ever in need of balance. We're either jauntily talking about what we will or will not say when we meet the holy God, or we're afraid to even hint that we'll be graciously received by him for the sake of Christ our Savior. Some of us assume a breezy familiarity with "our good friend, God," while others have never come to trust the love of God toward them in Jesus Christ.

This much we know: *Forgiveness of sins is essential to life with God, but the unbroken awareness of being forgiven is not!*

I have a friend who gave her life to Jesus Christ many years ago. She's far from sinless, but she works for him each day until she's tired; she prays and does all those other things that we would expect of one who has made Jesus her Lord. She can quote all the texts on the saving love and grace of God, and it is completely foreign to her that she could earn salvation. But she can find no permanent inner peace.[2] She is rarely free from the fear that she is not accepted in Christ.

We've been through the Story and exegeted texts together to no avail. It would be easy to guess at the problem and the cure. It isn't the Word of Christ she doubts. It's herself. I've often thought, "This time, we can settle it"; but no.

If I don't long for him . . . I *long* to long for him. If I don't love him . . . I *want* to love him. If I don't serve him . . . I *desire* to serve him.

I wish she could feel confidence and peace in the presence of God through Christ, but she may never experience it in this life. I've recently assured her that I'd rather she sought to please him—as she does—without the psychological appropriation of her salvation, than have her depart from him because she can't yet rejoice in him.

Who knows why we can't appropriate all he offers us? Do we feel our sin too intensely? Do we disparage our labor for him too much? Is it a question of emotional makeup? Childhood experiences? Rejection suffered at the hands of God's friends? Intellectual ignorance of Scripture? Intimidation by the flippant assurance of others. Who knows? God does!

Tell me my relationship with my family and friends is in need of improvement, and I'll agree. Tell me I have no relationship with them, that I have no love for them; and I'll profoundly disagree. Tell me my relationship with God is in dire need of enrichment, cleansing, strengthening, and commitment; and I'll agree. Tell me I don't care for him at all, and I'll deny it with every fiber in my being.

If I don't long for him . . . I *long* to long for him. If I don't love him . . . I *want* to love him. If I don't serve him . . . I *desire* to serve him.

In his first epistle, John stresses the life of love that is expected of God's people. He stresses that there is a line between those who are of God and those who are of the World Hater. When he calls for love of one another, he calls for it on the basis of God's love for us—and *that* is enough to make a sensitive heart nervous.

Having called his fellow-disciples to a love that is more than words, he says,

> If we live like this, we shall know that we are children of the truth and can reassure ourselves in the sight of God, even if our own hearts make us feel guilty. For God is infinitely greater than our hearts, and he knows everything. And if, dear friends of mine, when we realize this our hearts no longer accuse us, we may have the utmost confidence in God's presence.[3]

If you know that you love him and his people, even while you acknowledge the need for vast improvement, you can quieten your accusing heart, which reminds you of your sinfulness. God knows all your heart knows—and more—and it is to those whose hearts are accusing them that John speaks the word of assurance.

Doubt your doubts, and trust in the love God has for you.

♦

✦

Isn't Somebody Going to Forgive Me?

The boy had broken something very valuable, and as I recall, he was blaming it on someone else. His parents called all the staff into the large library room and began the investigation, which in the end, showed the boy to be the culprit. Now exposed, apologetic, ashamed, and surrounded by a roomful of adults who stood silent and looking at him, he began to cry and then said in a heartbreaking tone, "Isn't somebody going to forgive me?"

I *know* it isn't helpful to act as if there are no wrongs to forgive. I know it isn't right to whitewash our wickedness—but for the penitent heart, filled with remorse, there must be full, free, glad *forgiveness!*

FOUR:

The God

Who

Forgives

Sins

♦

100

Of course, we can't create anguish for people and then expect them to dispense forgiveness as though they were slot machines—apology in, forgiveness automatically given. A broken spirit and a contrite heart won't treat the sinned-against ones like that.

Just the same, we need to criticize "the ugly temper that tells us we had better continue to make the wrong-doer cringe and grovel. So conscious of our wounded dignity . . . we would rather hold to our implacable temper than have him say he's sorry. . . . It's utterly hateful to God, this way we have of being hard in a calm way to people who may have injured us."[1]

It's too easy to play God, too easy to find reasons to withhold the restoration of full fellowship. To the impenitent who don't feel the need for forgiveness, our isolating them or giving them the cold shoulder means nothing. It's the remorseful and penitent who are like a mass of exposed nerve endings—it's these who need our fellowship; it's these who agonize at every cold look, every flat and toneless word. They weep when they're alone and writhe in agony at the memory of your cool "hello" and "goodbye" when they tried to engage you in conversation earlier in the day.

And the trouble is, you see, they can't enjoy the forgiveness God has freely given them, because you, we, make them doubt it. They haven't the strength or assurance to live in the joy and freedom of a gracious God's free-flowing grace.

And isn't his forgiving us just that—free-flowing and gracious? Doesn't the story of the Prodigal make it appear so easy? Doesn't it seem to say that the forgiveness could not be more freely given, even if it had cost the father (the Father) absolutely nothing? How unlike us, sad to say.

There are those who have forgiven us but who have made it clear how costly it all was. They cannot give it graciously; it must be made to appear difficult; we must be made aware that our sin has pressed the very limits of a human—it was just about all the forgiver could do to be reconciled with us. And the more they talk, the less persuaded we are that forgiveness is possible with them.

If they acted as though a fine meal they were giving us was so burdensome, we could hardly bear to eat: an endless parade of the cost, the time and energy spent, the heat of the kitchen, the preparations, the shopping, the burned fingers, the press of time. By the time they were finished, we'd be tempted to treat the meal as David treated the water brought to him from the well at Bethlehem—too sacred to eat or drink.

Isn't

Somebody

Going to

Forgive

Me?

♦

101

They can't enjoy the forgiveness God has freely given them because we make them doubt it.

It isn't so with God. Like a gracious host, says Forsyth, he doesn't tediously go on about the cost of forgiveness. Though the awful cost is real, he allows us, as we mature, to gradually see more and more clearly the nature of our sin and the lengths to which he has gone to forgive.[2]

Yes, there is someone who will forgive us! As we stand in humble penitence, in terrible need, tearfully asking, "Isn't somebody going to forgive me?" God rises up with a warm, though wounded heart, takes us to himself and says, "I will. I will forgive you."

"Against you, you only, have I sinned and done what is evil in your sight."

—Psalm 51:4

◆

Of Judges and Friends

Whatever it takes! We need to do or say whatever it takes to be done with sinning. Jesus was so serious about it that he passionately urged people to cut off offending hands or feet or gouge out erring eyes in order that life might not be lost.[1]

Under and by the grace of God, we need to *enlist the emotions* in the war against sin and in the service of what's honorable. The intellect is never strong enough to sustain us in a war for the right, and while we mustn't sideline or despise rationality, there must be an appeal to affection, loyalty, and other noble qualities in the ongoing clash with evil.

FOUR:

The God

Who

Forgives

Sins

◆

104

This is part of the reason we must see our relationship with God as one of holy *friendship* as well as Creator/creature, Judge/judged, Master/servant.

To speak of God as *friend* puts our violations of his good and holy will into a much-needed perspective. "Judge," while it is right and proper, doesn't enlist our emotions in the service of holiness. "Judge," while it is true and necessary, doesn't feed our passions and warm our blood. We "break the law," and the Judge reacts as a judge. We immediately feel that breaking a law is different from breaking a friend's heart. I drive fifty in a thirty-limit area, get caught, and pay the fine—no big deal. I didn't know the policeman or the judge as persons, and I had no emotional attachment to the statute—it was all virtually impersonal. I broke nobody's heart, disappointed no one, so I suffer no emotional trauma.

A law is "only a law" until it is the heart's desire of my friend. Then it becomes something else. Then it enlists my affections. It makes it more difficult and, on some rare occasions, virtually impossible to break the "law."

A law is "only a law" until it is the heart's desire of my friend.

Isn't there someone in your life against whom you will not speak a slanderous word—someone against whom you couldn't be *forced* to speak a slanderous word or do a treacherous deed? Of course! And why is this so?

Tell me, why is this so?

However you answer, somewhere in there will be something about loving that person, something about friendship and warmth. The emotions of the relationship are so powerful that not only is there no conscious act of betrayal, there doesn't even arise a conscious thought of betrayal. Isn't this so! Haven't we experienced such a thing in our own very lives, and haven't we seen such a thing in others!

And should it be, in some moment of strong temptation, in an area in which we are especially weak, that we do something at that friend's expense, doesn't there follow a wave of shame and remorse that simply engulfs us?

"What would be said of a man," asks Hugh Mackintosh, "who came to neglect or deceive or hate or calumniate the kindest lifelong friend, and who, when the facts were pointed out to him, replied, 'Well, that doesn't worry me in the least'? What should we think of ourselves if we had done this? But we have done it. It is the very meaning of sin. . . . Sin is turning our back in scorn on all that God has been for us."[2]

Sin takes on a different aura when we see it as a violation of friendship and not merely a violation of law. When we "break a law," there are powerful words and feelings that *don't* come into play. Words like treachery, betrayal, cowardice, and selfishness. On the other hand, if we adhere to the law, we will easily speak of our being "law abiding" but not of loyalty, affection, devotion, friendship, or love.

It's important for us, then, to see our relationship with God in terms of friendship. Christ called his disciples his friends, and God called Abraham his friend.[3] It's important for us to do this in our war against sin and in our pursuit of holiness, because *we need more than laws to help us keep laws.* We must see the laws as related to a *relationship* with God, a relationship that has in it a holy affection.

And if we do, it will affect us in our direct response to God and in our indirect response to him through how we

FOUR:

The God

Who

Forgives

Sins

♦

106

treat his children. To seriously hurt my friend, says Mackintosh, will mean that tension will arise in our relationship.[4] But what if we hurt his much-loved children?

To sin against God's own is to sin against God.

But all that is the sober side of the matter—the essentially sober side of the matter. To see sin in the light of friendship shows its ugliness with special clarity, but it shows forgiveness with special clearness also.

The blacker we see sin to be, the harder it is for us to see how it could be forgiven. That's why in our better moments we can hardly believe for joy what the psalmist said: "With you there is forgiveness."[5] There is not only a God there to whom we can say, "God be merciful to me the sinner," there is one there who is merciful and forgiving.

What is it that helps us believe in God's mercy? We can believe because in our tiny little lives we have known people who have forgiven us, people we hurt in the worst possible way, people we hurt with a deliberateness and callousness—to the extent that we were sure they would never again have anything to do with us. And yet they refused to let our actions be the ultimate reality. They robbed our wrongs of their divisive power, robbed them of their power to eternally separate us—and at great cost, since they bear the agony of our loveless deed(s) and since they take the initiative that results in forgiveness.

And if our fellow sinners, touched by the heart of God, can do that for us, surely God is willing. If our earthly friends and parents can rise to this wondrous height, should we not think noble things of our heavenly Father and friend?

✦

Ruby Bridges

But isn't the whole topic for "sissies"? And isn't all this forgiveness business "softness"? Isn't it "easy"?

Soft? Try it! Do it! Forgive an agonizing wrong, or a series of agonizing wrongs, done to you or to one you love; forgive it with a glad-hearted, full forgiveness, and then tell us how soft it is. Only the strong can do such a thing!

Easy? We hear much of difficult choices, difficult undertakings, and costly moves in the area of evangelism or benevolence. Praise God for them! To survive on one meager meal a day for years, to trek for hours or days through difficult terrain to preach the gospel, to burn one's eyes out in endless study to God's glory—all this

FOUR:

The God

Who

Forgives

Sins

◆

108

may be difficult, but no more so than to live in a forgiving mode. To always make the moves to bring about reconciliation, to confront and plead while bearing the agony of the wrong—*that's* difficult.

Right at the beginning of the 1960s, a young psychiatrist, Robert Coles, now one of America's leading child psychiatrists and best-selling authors, came across six-year-old Ruby Bridges in New Orleans. The United States government had just ordered the desegregation of the schools, and Coles saw this little black girl being escorted into the Franz Elementary School by federal marshals while the streets were lined with screaming, threatening, cursing people, held back—but only just— by the local police. Ruby was the only student at the school. Coles began to talk to the teacher and to visit the Bridges' home a couple of times a week.

To always make the moves to bring about reconciliation, to confront and plead while bearing the agony of the wrong—*that's* difficult.

"Today I thought of you," said the teacher to Coles. "I was looking out of the window, and she stopped right in front of that mob. It was the first time she's ever done that. She started talking. They went wild; they surged toward her; they were going to get her. The marshals had to draw their guns. The marshals were pulling at her to get her into the building, and she wouldn't move. She kept talking, and they screamed louder and louder, and finally she stopped, and they got her in the building. They said to her, 'Don't do that again.'

"So I said to her, 'Ruby what did you say to them?'"

"She said to me, 'I didn't say anything to them.'"

"And then I said to her, 'Well, I saw your lips moving; you must have said something to them.'"

"She said, 'I didn't say anything to them.'"

The teacher decided not to pursue the matter any further, but to let Coles deal with it, since he was due to go to her house that evening.

In the kitchen that evening, Coles and Ruby talked while she drew. He asked her how she was doing, and she said she was doing fine.

"I know you're doing fine, Ruby, but I heard something today that worried me and worried your teacher."

"What was that?" she wanted to know.

"You said something to the mob that got the marshals and the teacher upset . . . were you upset?"

"I wasn't upset," she said.

"You said something to those people that got them upset."

"I didn't say anything to those people . . . I was saying a prayer."

"You were saying a prayer?" Coles echoed, "What kind of prayer?"

"A prayer for those people."

"Why would you want to say a prayer for those people . . . after all the terrible things you've heard from them?"

"Don't you think they need a prayer?"

"Yes," said Coles slowly. "What was this prayer about?"

"I always pray the same thing."

"What's that?"

"Please, God, try to forgive these people because they don't know what they're doing."

FOUR:

The God

Who

Forgives

Sins

♦

110

Coles remarked later that even in his secular mind, he had remembered hearing that somewhere before.

When the full story was told, he learned that Ruby had an arrangement with the marshals that she would stop several blocks from the school, pray, and then go on. That particular morning, she had forgotten to pray and only remembered just before she went into the building.[1]

And why had she begun to pray such a prayer? Her parents were share-cropping stock from Mississippi. Neither of them could read or write; her father worked as a janitor, and her mother scrubbed offices at night. But they taught their daughter that Christ prayed that prayer when he was facing a mob that was screaming at him.

It must have been hard for them to see their little girl head out each morning to face the gauntlet of viciousness and hatred, to have to listen to the obscenities and threats. "Ignorant" they may have been, but not in the ways of courage and sacrifice.

And I'm sure you're wondering how God might have felt as he watched his boy facing his own gauntlet on his way to Golgotha.

> *"If we claim to be without sin, we deceive ourselves and the truth is not in us. If we confess our sins, he is faithful and just and will forgive us our sins and purify us from all unrighteousness."*
>
> —1 John 1:8–9

✦

Humans Need Forgiving

Ted Turner, the rich and powerful communications magnate, wanted to make his views clear. Did Jesus Christ die for his sins? "He needn't have bothered," said Turner, who felt and feels no need of forgiveness. This man, incredibly blessed by God in all kinds of ways, speaks for a growing segment of the blessed. They'll apologize to each other for not holding the door open, apologize for spilling some food or drink, apologize for keeping the other waiting, and even apologize for things they had no part in ("I'm sorry Harriet treated you that way")—but apologize to God? Never! Do they feel the

FOUR:

The God

Who

Forgives

Sins

♦

112

need of forgiveness for cheapening themselves and others as they dishonor God? No sir!

While there are many like Turner who don't see "sin" as any kind of issue *really* worth talking about (unless it takes a form that violates Mr. Turner's rights, in which case he bellows about greed, crookedness, and the like), there are millions with better vision who agree with Maxwell:

> There are things worse than trouble, worse than pain, worse than death. Sin, to God, is the only unendurable, more intolerable even than hell. Yes, God hates hell, hates it more than we do, but He hates sin more than He hates hell. If all the world's mounting miseries will crowd men to Christ and make hell the emptier, they are better than sin . . . thistles, thorns, sweat— better than sin. Sorrows, sickness, suffering— better than sin. Pain, poverty, affliction—better than sin.
>
> Wars, plagues, famines, disease, destruction, death—better than sin. Endless tyranny, unpitied tears, broken hearts—better than sin.
>
> "Ashes to ashes, dust to dust" our "mortal coil destined to the invasion of a million worms"— *all better than sin!*[1]

This is frighteningly true! And it is true not only because sin dishonors the sovereign and holy Lord of the universe, it's true because the bulk of all our heartache, disease, famine, and poverty results from our sinful treatment of ourselves and one another.

Forgiveness is needed—felt or not!

✦

God Delights in Forgiving!

God is no CPA who keeps a check on every call for pardon! Isaiah 40–66 sees Israel in captivity and longing to get right with God and back home, and this is what God calls them to: He urges them to turn from idolatry and to trust in him where they'll find the hunger of their souls satisfied. If only they will turn from their wicked schemes and trust themselves to him whom they have so treacherously betrayed, they will find to their surprise that he will *abundantly* pardon![1]

"Abundantly pardon." The Jerusalem Bible describes God as "rich in forgiving."[2] Isn't that good news? The flow of forgiveness from God to man is unhindered, like

113

water pouring over the falls at Niagara—free-flowing and abundant.

A servant owed his master an amount of money that he couldn't possibly repay, but when he was called to pay it, he pleaded for mercy and time, assuring the master that he would repay every cent. The master was filled with pity for him and did more than he was asked—he forgave the millions of dollars owed.[3] Jesus told this story to illustrate the kind of abundant forgiveness God practices and wants his servants to practice.

♦

The flow of forgiveness from God to man is unhindered, like water pouring over the falls at Niagara—free-flowing and abundant.

∾

But God not only offers an abundance of forgiveness, he offers it with *delight!* Here's how one prophet put it:

> Where else is a God like you,
>   who forgives transgression and passes over
>   wrong?
> For the sake of his people's survivors
>   he does not store his anger forever,
>   but *delights* in showing mercy.
> He will come back, he will pity us,
>   he will trample our sins under his feet.
>   Yes, you will cast all our sins into the depths
>   of the sea;
> you will show your faithfulness to Jacob,
>   your true love to Abraham,
> as you have sworn to our fathers, from the
>   days of long ago.[4]

Notice how the prophet, with awe in his voice, extols God—not for creating galaxies with a word or constellations with a sigh, but for the delight he finds in forgiving!

Joy is a deeper word than *delight*. Delight speaks more of the emotion as it shows; it's more surface. And for this very reason it's wonderful to find it in this passage. The Hebrew word stresses the emotional involvement. God is "tickled pink" (maybe that isn't irreverent) to extend forgiveness. It isn't just a deep, satisfying pleasure, it is a *delight*. (Think about the prodigal in Luke 15.)

Delight is what a schoolboy feels when, having won his own event in the track meet, he sees his best friend (I mean his *very* best friend) win his also. It's what the young girl feels when the young man she adores flashes an excited smile and the engagement ring they spoke of in whispers days before. It's what the husband feels when he, quite accidentally, overhears people tell one another of the graciousness of his wife. And it's what the little girl feels when her friends ooh and aah over her dad as he drops her off at school ("What a fox," they say).

It's what God feels when we give him the chance to forgive us.

✦

No Fishing!

I've no doubt we sing it too easily—without thinking of it deeply enough. We sing,

> My sin—Oh, the bliss of this glorious
>   thought—
> My sin, not in part but the whole,
> Is nailed to the cross and I bear it no more:
> Praise the Lord, praise the Lord, O my soul![1]

We can't always appreciate that truth, but it's always true. In our better moments, when we are more in tune with our lives and his grace, we love the song and the truth it joyfully proclaims.

FOUR:

The God

Who

Forgives

Sins

♦

118

God forgives *completely!* *There are no sins,* hidden or forgotten, that will be dragged out on that awesome and coming Day that will threaten our relationship with God. He didn't forget them, and they weren't hidden from him. *There are no sins,* scarlet, stark, gross or otherwise, that are set to the side to be mulled over later by the sovereign Lord. They're covered, forgiven! *There are no sins,* of commission *or* omission, that will spoil the joy on that thrilling Day of even *one* of those who are among the multiplied millions of God's people down the ages. He cleanses them from *all* unrighteousness.[2]

John Donne in his *A Hymn to God the Father* spoke our fear, our prayer, and our assurance this way:

> Wilt thou forgive that sin where I begun,
>   Which is my sin, though it were done before?
> Wilt thou forgive those sins, through which I run,
>   And do run still: though still I do deplore?
>   When Thou has done, thou hast not done,
>   For, I have more.
>
> I have a sin of fear, that when I have spun
>   My last thread, I shall perish on the shore;
> Swear by thy self, that at my death thy son
>   Shall shine as he shines now, and heretofore;
>   And, having done that, Thou hast done,
>   I fear no more.[3]

Not only is God's forgiveness absolutely complete, it is also *permanent!* "I will forgive their wickedness and will remember their sins no more" is how Jeremiah puts it.[4] Corrie Ten Boom enjoyed saying that God casts our sins into the deepest part of the ocean and then puts up a sign: *No Fishing!* I like that.

It isn't that God doesn't "remember" what we've done. Of course he does. Can't he read the biblical record as well as we? Didn't he have the story of David's failures put down? And Peter's? No, the promise means he doesn't remember them *against* us so that they cut us off from him.

The Hebrew writer not only makes full use of the passage from Jeremiah 31, he insists, "When this priest had offered for all time one sacrifice for sins, he sat down at the right hand of God. . . . Because by one sacrifice he has made perfect forever those who are being made holy."[5]

To his sinful people the holy and gracious God has this to say, "I, even I, am he who blots out your transgressions, for my own sake, and remembers your sins no more."[6]

It isn't that God doesn't "remember" our sins; it's that he doesn't remember them *against* us.

∞

God is no dog that keeps digging up old bones. Think noble things of him! He may chastise us for our sins, but he will not keep bringing them up. *Others* may do that, *we* may even do that, but God won't. And it's this, in the end, that is of ultimate importance to us. What others think, what we think, doesn't really matter. There is one Lord, and he has given us the gift of complete, free, permanent forgiveness. That's why Wilbur Rees, in his *$3 Worth of God,* has one of his characters triumphantly say to the hard-hearted critic,

> You are impressive, Your Honor. You sit there in your long black robe belching hell from your puffed lips. You are judgement incarnate. Your

blazing eyes are enough to burn mercy to a cinder. You have enough evidence stacked up to send me to the chair. You are everywhere: behind the pulpit, across the fence, in the front office. You condemn me with a knowing look and try me with a raised eyebrow. Your mission is to punish, to shackle, to damn. What you don't know is that I've got the Governor's reprieve in my hip pocket. You can't hurt me. I can stare you down. I can laugh at your pomposity. You've just lost your jurisdiction.[7]

♦

> *"It was not with perishable things such as silver or gold that you were redeemed from the empty way of life, but with the precious blood of Christ, a lamb without blemish or defect."*
>
> —1 Peter 1:18–19

✦

Jesus Paid It All!

"Jesus paid it all" is true! *Of course* we must appropriate it on his terms, or we have no forgiveness; but that changes nothing! Sinners in the New Testament appropriated this free gift by identifying themselves with Jesus Christ in whom, and in whom alone, there is life and forgiveness. Thousands gladly received the good news and took his name on themselves.

But it never entered their minds that they were *earning* anything!

Forgiveness, and the life of which forgiveness is a part, cannot be bought or earned or seized! Nothing we offer or do can pay any part of the ransom price!

FOUR:

The God

Who

Forgives

Sins

♦

122

Jesus paid it all!

True, unless we become his followers, there is no forgiveness; but our coming to him is not meritorious! We have no merit! We come to *him* because *we* can't handle the sin problem. Man's obedience has no buying power, no covering power, no redeeming power.

A pauper looking in the window of a jewelry store sees the most incredible jewel imaginable. The owner, seeing his adoring gaze, catches his eye and beckons him to come in.

"Would you like to have this?" he asks the pauper.

"But it's probably priceless," the impoverished man replies.

"You're right. But you can have it for nothing," the store owner says.

"You don't understand," says the penniless man. "I don't have any money. I can't possibly pay for it."

"*You* don't understand," he's told. "It's already been paid for. I'm offering it as a gift, free for the taking."

The pauper searches his pockets and produces a nickel and two pennies. He thinks of offering them in payment, but knows instinctively that however it might make him feel, it would be a colossal insult to the owner. He puts them back in his pocket under the owner's approving gaze.

Either it is a gift that he will accept as a gift, or he won't get it!

With eyes shining and heart leaping, but hardly believing that such a wonder is his, for free, he puts out his hand and accepts it. Further examination reveals it to be even more lovely than he knew, and in hushed, thankful tones he says, "It must have cost someone a lot!"

"It did indeed," whispered the owner.

◆

Why Must You Die?

"For God did not send his Son into the world to condemn the world . . . ."[1]

And why not? Because we didn't need any help from God to get that done. We'd done a perfect job on that already. Condemnation wasn't what we needed; we already had that. What we needed was something else.

"For God did not send his Son into the world to condemn the world, *but to save the world through him.*"[2]

Of course there are those who care nothing that Christ has come! That they shrug when they hear the Story is sad, but that's how it is. They go their way to destruction with their eyes wide open (or as wide open as spiritual

FOUR:

The God

Who

Forgives

Sins

♦

124

lunacy will allow). It's a terrible tragedy that people choose eternal lostness; but maybe it's an even greater tragedy that there are millions who think they have no alternative.

People are running past Jesus in their multiplied thousands and throwing themselves into the abyss of destruction.

"Why are you doing this?" he asks.

"Because we're sinners," they shout over their shoulder on the way to perdition.

"But why must you die?" the Savior sorrowfully asks.

"Because we're sinners, we tell you, and God wants us to perish."

"But," says the Savior, "I'm God, and I don't want you to perish!"

It's a terrible tragedy that people choose eternal lostness; but maybe it's an even greater tragedy that there are millions who think they have no alternative.

"You mean we don't have to go to destruction?" they ask in astonishment.

"Why, no!" says the Master.

"Then we aren't going," say they with joy.

"Good for you," smiles the Christ. "Now, stand beside me and tell all these others they don't have to go either."

THE God

OF THE TOWEL

· FIVE ·

✦

Twelve Lords, One Servant

There were thirteen men in an upper room—how many servants and how many lords? "One Lord and twelve servants" sounds like the right answer, but is it? The truth is there were twelve lords and one Servant! Only one man in the room knew anything about service.

In the end, that's why he was made Lord. Down through the centuries, God has given power to many men and women; but only one really knew how to use it.

When Jesus was a little boy, God gave him some power and influence over his peers, and Jesus used it to do them good. And God watched him with growing interest. Then he gave him power to understand Scripture and saw him use it in the temple for his Father's honor. Later still, he gave him power over bread, and he fed people; he gave him power over disease, and he healed people; he gave him power over death, and he raised people; he gave him power over sin, and he forgave people. And God watched it all with admiration, knowing that here, finally, was a human who knew what to do with power from God—he blessed and redeemed people! So God gave him power over his own life.[1] And what did he do? He laid his life down for others! No wonder the Father said of him, "This is my Son, whom I love; with him I am well pleased."[2]

And because Jesus not only knew what power was for, because he *did* with it what God wanted done, God knew he could trust him with all power and gave it to him.

We mustn't think that Jesus the Christ has all authority just because he's *greater* than us; he has all authority because he's *better* than us.

We mustn't think that Jesus the Christ has all authority just because he's *greater* than us; he has all authority because he's *better* than us.

Paul expressly links Jesus' lordship with his servanthood! Here's what he says,

> Your attitude should be the same as that of Christ Jesus:
>
> Who, being in very nature God,
>   did not consider equality with God
>   something to be grasped,

but made himself nothing,
 taking the very nature of a servant,
 being made in human likeness.
And being found in appearance as a man, *Twelve*
 he humbled himself
 and became obedient to death— *Lords,*
  even death on a cross!
Therefore God exalted him to the highest place *One*
 and gave him the name that is above
  every name, *Servant*
that at the name of Jesus every knee should bow,
 in heaven and on earth and under
  the earth,
and every tongue confess that Jesus Christ ♦
 is Lord,
 to the glory of God the Father.[3]

"Therefore, God exalted him to the highest place!" 129
Why? Because it was in Jesus' heart to humble himself for the eternal help of those unable to help themselves.

I watched her, this critic of the Christian faith, scorn truths that millions hold precious, and in the course of it she said, "Why should we praise God? If I were God, I could do the things God can do!" Just so. But whether people wish to believe it or not, the Christian's Story is that God, in Jesus Christ, became as human as this lady was and *still* did better than she (or anyone else) has done. So it isn't simply a matter of power or brute force; it's a matter of goodness and lovingkindness.

But so that we have this clear, let me make the point: the young man in the upper room who wore the towel and served others was the incarnate God. The visible acts of service sprang from the heart of this young man, but there's more to it than that.

What Jesus did in this human realm was in keeping with who he was in that other realm. Before the upper room, before the stable at Bethlehem, there was the glory of godhood, there was the position of majesty; he was worshiped by angels and all creation. But Paul insists that along with all this there was a *servant's heart!*

Because there was such a heart, there came a time when the one we now know as Jesus of Nazareth called a halt to the worship he was worthy of and took his place among the worshipers. The majesty, the power, the glory, the worship—the prerogatives of godhood were laid aside as he robed himself in *humanity.*

"Jesus . . . got up from the meal, took off his outer clothing, and wrapped a towel around his waist. After that, he poured water into a basin and began to wash his disciples' feet, drying them with the towel that was wrapped around him."

—John 13:4–5

✦

God Is Not Slumming

God is not slumming when he serves! It is part of his character. The only God we know, the only true God, has a serving heart.

But the idea of a God with a servant's heart sets off alarm bells within many of us. We think of God mainly in terms of *power,* and we find it hard to get around the notion that *power* and *service* are like oil and water. Nor do we find it easy to get around the notion that serving is humiliating. Peter, too, found a *serving* Lord hard to comprehend.

And so when the Christ knelt before his disciples and began to wash their feet, Peter watched anxiously. Closer and closer Jesus came, until it looked as if he were going to wash Peter's too. "Lord, are you going to wash my feet?" he burst out. The Master speaks, but Peter hotly refused to be talked around. Messiahs don't act like that; leaders don't lower themselves this way; lords aren't servants. "No, you shall never wash my feet," he cried.

The Master must have fixed him with those big eyes of his: "Unless I wash you, you have no part with me," he murmured.

Honest Peter was offended by the Master's servanthood, embarrassed by a Messiah on his knees; it was all too much for him. Whatever else he knew or didn't know, he knew his Master was *serving,* and a serving Lord wasn't to his liking. He saw the incongruity of who Jesus was and what he was doing.

What the Christ said to him, as I understand him, was this: "What you see is what you get. This is the kind of Messiah I am, and if you reject the spirit you are seeing here and want none of it, so be it. If you don't want this, you don't want me; for this is what I *am,* not just what I *do."* This wasn't a *threat* so much as a declaration of fact. If Peter rejected servanthood in his view of lordship, he could have no part with this Lord hunkering down before him. Peter saw a gulf between service and lordship; but for Christ, there was none!

It doesn't matter that it offends Peter's (or our) sensibilities; God has, as part of his character, the longing to serve. It isn't unlike him. And we must resist to the death the idea that the serving spirit in God *began* with the incarnation. No, it's what *led* to the incarnation! The incarnation was the visible expression of what was always a part of godhood.

Some years ago a man came to me quite distressed by such teaching. We had a long discussion in which he made his case. He thought by saying such things, I was cheapening God. My final offering was, "How can I dishonor God by telling people what he said about himself? What he *did?* If God hadn't wanted us to say such things, he shouldn't have *done* such things." He couldn't receive this and gave his reasons for it. But I thought I heard again (perhaps I'm wrong)—I thought I heard again, Peter protesting in an upper room at his Lord acting as his servant.

Wilbur Rees caught the scandal of it perfectly when he has one of his characters say,

> Your king lacks class! No one will follow him. A king has to have flare and style. He has to arouse feelings of pride and prestige. People have to identify with him. They must be able to say, "His prowess is my prowess and his glory is my glory!" He has to have dignity and a certain aloofness. He has to know how to carry his crown and flash his sword in the sun. The least a king can do for his subjects is ride a spirited steed! What will you answer when men ask for your king? "He's over there on that ass with his sandals dragging on the ground." Ha! I'll lay you ten to one no one will ever follow him![1]

I wish I'd written that! What I'd like to stress in addition to that is this: the one who rides a donkey, feet dragging in the dirt, is not just a lovely Galilean carpenter whom God is making king. He is the incarnate God! What this young man is doing is revealing the heart—not just of a noble young human—but the heart of God.

> *"Jesus knew that the time had come for him to leave this world and go to the Father. Having loved his own who were in the world, he now showed them the full extent of his love."*
>
> —John 13:1

◆

With Love and Forethought

What was on his mind the night before they took him out, railroaded, and murdered him? The Scripture tells us he had a number of things on his mind. Telling us over and over what "Jesus knew," John wants the reader to understand that Christ does what he does in light of his knowing and *loving.*[1]

Jesus knew that the hour he had come into the world to meet had finally arrived[2]—the hour of betrayal, the hour of incredible inner turmoil, the hour of national rejection and sin-bearing.

Jesus knew that the Father had unchangeably purposed to give all authority and control to him[3]—authority beyond the wildest dreams of the greatest megalomaniac.

Jesus knew that he had come out from God[4]—he was fully aware of his divine *origin.* He had understood this even as a twelve-year-old boy, and a short but full life had not shaken that conviction—rather, it had strengthened it.

Jesus knew he was going back to the Father[5]—this was his divine *destination.* He knew he faced treachery, humiliation, desertion, and the Cross, but he also knew that he would return to glory with his Father.

In light of all this, knowing all this, and having loved his disciples from the beginning until now—what did he do? *He acted out servanthood!*

Aren't we tempted here to feel disappointed? Yes, yes, servanthood is lovely and all that, humility is grand, but in a world like theirs, a world like ours, isn't there a need for *power?* For vigor and authority? In the face of entrenched evil, powerful wickedness, strong criminals, and successful gangsters, shouldn't we be hearing about *power?* Shouldn't the example be of boldness and courage and explosive judgment. True, John Wayne let people push him around for a while; but before long, there were bodies lying everywhere—as *might* was used for right. Is this too much to ask from Christ? Does he have to link servanthood with thoughts about God and authority? But he knew what he was doing, didn't he!

I'm sure we don't object to occasional acts of service from Christ. I'm sure we quite admire them. What bothers us, at times, is that he seems to make servanthood a part of the *character* of God. It isn't just something God *does,* it's who he is.

And down inside we have the sinking feeling that that is what he calls us to. Believing that doing acts of service is required of us is one thing; believing we are to *be* servants is something else altogether.

> *"Then I saw a Lamb, looking as if it had been slain,*
> *standing in the center of the throne."*
> —Revelation 5:6

✦

The Lamb at the Center of the Throne

Revelation 5 tells us that in the center of the throne that ruled the universe was a self-surrendered *Lamb*—a Lamb that had suffered death but that now *stood,* very much alive, though bearing the marks of having been slaughtered.

This passage in Revelation teaches us that not only does God *redeem* us in terms of the "suffering servant," Jesus Christ, but that he *rules* in terms of that servant. Christ was not only at the heart of the *Cross;* he was at the heart of the *throne.*

To Pilate, the Master said, "My kingdom is not of this world. If it were, my servants would fight to prevent my arrest by the Jews. But now my kingdom is from another place."[1]

What did he mean by "My kingdom [royal power] is not of this world"? He couldn't have meant he doesn't rule the world, because he does.[2] He couldn't have meant he only ruled spirits, that he doesn't rule people, kings, or nations, because he *does* rule nations and kings.[3] What did he mean, "My kingdom [royal authority] is not of this world"?

He certainly meant his authority wasn't gained by physical violence, however justified it could be made to appear. If it was, he said, his servants would have taken up arms to free him. His kingly power was unearthly! Unworldly! His power was different from Rome's. "Rome creates a desert and calls it peace."[4] The emperors, consuls, proconsuls, and the rest got their power through lies, murder, intrigue, and cruelty. They gained theirs by asserting themselves; he gained his by denying himself. They obtained theirs by destruction; he obtained his by redemption. Theirs was procured by defending themselves against all attackers; his he acquired by making himself vulnerable. They derived power by depending on themselves; he got his by depending on Another. They gained glory by making a name for themselves in war; he reached his by making himself of no reputation in an incarnation. They grasped and seized theirs to sate their lust for power; he accepted his to satisfy love for, and service to, people. The only blood he shed was his own.

"Into a tired old world," said the Dutch theologian Berkouwer, "where accounts must always be settled and old scores paid off, entered at long last One who did not demand blood for blood"[5]—*the Lamb at the center of the throne!*

> *"Whoever wishes to be great among you must be your servant . . .
> just as the Son of Man came not to be served but to serve."*
> —Matthew 20:26–28 NRSV

✦

Power: Pagan and Christ-like

Because he refused to enter with us into our clashing circles of pride and power-broking selfishness, Jesus is not only our Judge but our judgment. Where we grab and hoard, he earned and shared. He came, he said, to serve by giving his life as a ransom. The Father gave him *all* power, because every time he gave him *some,* he used it to bless others. He is our judgment, because he stamps every desire for power that isn't a desire to honor God and serve people—he stamps it *Pagan!* And he brands every exercise of power over any group or individual that is not specifically an exercise of service to God's glory—he brands it *Pagan!*

From day one, power has been about making people do what you want them to do, right? That everyone else has the same vision of power means that they are wanting to make you do what they want done. It's the only way, isn't it? That's how the kings or great ones of the Gentiles did it—they "lorded it over" others, said Christ.[1] They elected themselves and imposed their will on others.

"Well, thank God, we live in a democracy where that can't happen," someone exclaims fervently. But that misses the point. Democracy, at its worst, is where a large segment of people band together to impose their will on the smaller band. A democracy can be just as pagan as an empire or a monarchy. The issue is the same: the imposition of authority.

I've no wish to become too sophisticated or too "Christian" here, but it really is a question of spirit and aim. What do the power seekers—whether they're individuals or groups, small bands or large masses—what do they have in mind and, equally important, what is their present practice?

Power is about making people do what you want them to do.

Jesus said to followers who were jockeying for positions of power while angry with others for doing the same, "You know that the rulers of the Gentiles lord it over them, and their great ones are tyrants over them. It will not be so among you; but whoever wishes to be great among you must be your servant . . . just as the Son of Man came not to be served but to serve, and to give his life a ransom for many."[2] You will rule by serving, he said, *"just as* the Son of Man. . . ." Their power was to be like his.

There are only two kinds of power or authority: pagan and Christ-like. One is seized and is self-serving; the other is bestowed and is other-serving. It doesn't matter whether the power is exercised within a democratic or imperial political structure—its paganism is revealed in its intention and its exercise. In some respects, rigging elections or stampeding the electorate can be just as effective as rolling into a capital city with enough fire power to level the world. Experienced demagogues, local or national, can do, without guns or bombs, what other nontalkers need weapons for.

In Matthew 20, the Son of Man is asking us: "How do you feel about those you wish to have power over. What do you mean to do *for* them? Are you willing to let *serving* them be your way of life and your credentials for 'office'? Will you allow your aim and practice to be your appeal to them?"

Power or authority that is *pagan* in essence need not be crassly stupid. Even tyrants know you have to cater to somebody, whether it's the secret police, the military, or the financially powerful. Granting privileges to certain ones in order to keep control and so serve your own ultimate agenda is no less pagan than rumbling tanks over the bodies of children—it's just another tactic in the campaign to gain power that has "Attila the Hun" branded all over it.

"It will not be so among you," said the Christ. Hmmmm.

"Let us not become weary in doing good, for at the proper time
we will reap a harvest if we do not give up."

—Galatians 6:9

✦

"Made a Difference to That One"

It's got to be a mistake to wait until we can do something grand before we act in service. In our better moments we all recognize that. And it's got to be a mistake to serve only in areas where we can see the end of the job rather than to get involved in an endeavor that stretches out before us and vanishes into the horizon. In our finer moments we shake our heads at such cost-counting.

But we aren't always in our better moments, and we aren't always in the grip of noble impulses. Sometimes we get fed up with jobs that never end; we have our fill of brave rushes that don't seem to make an impression, much less a dent in the "enemy" before us. We suffer compassion-fatigue; we begin to hear more clearly the whispering voices that say we're accomplishing nothing. And worse, we begin to agree with those voices, and a sense of despair descends on us.

Albert Schweitzer, the German theologian who became a missionary to Africa, understood the temptation to allow his feebleness to discourage him, but he thrust it from him decisively. "I never allow the magnitude of the task," he said, "to blind me or keep me from doing what I could to change things." Wise man. Strong man!

Jack Canfield and Mark Hansen in their book, *Chicken Soup for the Soul,* tell of a friend of theirs on a beach in Mexico. He saw a local man bending down and picking things up and throwing them into the water. They were starfish.

It's got to be a mistake to wait until we can do something grand before we act in service.

"What are you doing?" Hansen's friend asked.

"It's low tide, and if I don't get these starfish back into the water they'll die," said the man.

"But there are thousands of starfish up and down this beach and hundreds of beaches up and down the coast littered with starfish," said the visitor. "You must know you can't possibly make a difference."

The local man smiled, bent down, picked up another starfish, and threw it into the sea. "Made a difference to that one," he said.[1]

✦

Take My Word for It

They're terribly upset. He's talking about going away, and it makes no sense to them. Thomas confesses he doesn't know what his Master is talking about, and Philip asks to see the Father (wanting a theophany, perhaps, as Moses had asked for in Exodus 33). It was at this point that Jesus said, "Don't you know me, Philip, even after I have been among you such a long time? Anyone who has seen me has seen the Father. How can you say, 'Show us the Father'?"[1]

They wanted to see the glory of God, to know the person of God and his character. "If you really knew me, you would know my Father as well."[2] Why was it so hard for them to believe?

They thought—as we almost always think today—in terms of power, *almighty* power! When we're in pain, we lift our eyes to the one we believe has the power to change things. When we get in trouble, we look to him who has the power to get us out. When we see the pain, injustice, and chaos in the world, we pray to the one who parted seas and buried continents. We want a God with *power!*

So when they saw this Messiah of theirs enduring rejection, scorn, and threats; when they saw him putting up with so much that they wouldn't have put up with—how could they see him in terms of "God"?

He recognized it was difficult for them, but he asked them anyway, "Believe me when I say that I am in the Father and the Father is in me."[3] "Take my word for it," he is saying. "See my character, hear my teaching, note my purposes, and believe me when I tell you—when you look at me and know me, you are looking at God and knowing him."

He recognized it was difficult for them, but he asked them to believe anyway.

And then, in his gracious way, for those who struggle in the right direction, he makes allowances. "Or at least believe on the evidence of the miracles themselves."[4] This Christ of ours is no tyrant;[5] he understands that in a sinful world it isn't always easy for sinners to believe.

But he asks us, just the same, *"Take my word for it."*

✦

Only Half the Cure

A child and a distracted parent sought the Master's help as an unclean spirit tormented the child. "I beg you," said the nearly demented man; "look at my son, for he is my only child. A spirit seizes him and he suddenly screams; it throws him into convulsions so that he foams at the mouth. It scarcely ever leaves him and is destroying him." You can hear this father's pain, can't you? "It scarcely ever leaves him and is destroying him." This evil spirit had resisted the prayers of the apostolic group, but when Jesus speaks, the demon, in a final, spiteful throw, smashes the child to the ground before departing. That's when the onlooking crowd was "amazed at the greatness of God."[1] They saw the *power* of God and were astonished.

And it was while they were marveling at the power of God in Christ that Jesus said to the apostles, "Listen carefully to what I am about to tell you: The Son of Man is going to be betrayed into the hands of men."[2]

It doesn't really surprise us to learn that "they did not understand what this meant. It was hidden from them, so that they did not grasp it, and they were afraid to ask him about it."[3] They were feeling amazed at the power of God in Jesus, and all of a sudden, he starts talking about being betrayed into the hands of men. How is it possible for mere men to get their hands on someone like this? Even with the completed "script" in our hands, we still wrestle with the "weakness of omnipotence" and can't understand that *for a world needing redemption, having unlimited power is only half the cure.*

It's hard for us to understand that having unlimited power is only half the cure.

The brilliant preacher and professor of homiletics, Paul Scherer, rightly reminded us that there are some places where naked power cannot enter—one of them is the human heart.[4]

THE God

WHO ALLOWS SUFFERING

"Consider him who endured such opposition from sinful men, so that you will not grow weary and lose heart. In your struggle against sin, you have not yet resisted to the point of shedding your blood."

—Hebrews 12:3–4

✦

Hang Nails and Colon Cancers

You'll need to credit me with compassion before you read this section, for it might tempt you to think I'm callous. I can only assure you I don't feel that way, and if I display callousness, I renounce it as un-Christian and wish to be freed from it.

But I must admit that I'm weary of hearing people whine over things that are nothing more than inconveniences. I'm weary of hearing people drag God in for questioning because everything isn't going their way. I know from personal experience how easy it is to indulge in self-pity, but I don't like it in me and I'm not crazy about it in anybody else. Charlie Brown isn't alone.

SIX:

The God

Who

Allows

Suffering

♦

152

Charlie: "Nobody likes me. I mean nobody really likes me."

Friend: "I think I know how you feel, Charlie Brown. I think I know just how you must feel. You don't want pity. All you want is a little understanding."

Charlie: (with that I've-been-misunderstood look) "On the contrary. I'll take all the pity I can get."

We can talk ourselves into being bowls of jello. Some, by rambling on and on, indiscriminately, about how difficult life is and how many hard questions remain unanswered and how God owes us explanations and how tough it is to live here below with only a cottage—this going on and on can induce an *unholy discontent,* a "where are my rights?" disposition, and a marked self-centered agenda.

There is pain and pain, and there is suffering and suffering. To lump them all together is a blunder. A sprained ankle is painful, but who will call it pain in the presence of someone who has just received widespread, third-degree burns? Those who are afflicted with a case of the flu suffer, but who will speak of it as suffering in the presence of a victim of chronic asthma attacks or degenerative bone disease? There's a brand of suffering for those families who must *always* struggle, and struggle bravely, to make ends meet, but it pales to nothing when compared with those in countries like Haiti, Somalia, Albania, or elsewhere.

All this came home to me some time ago when Ethel met a friend of hers who had just suffered a series of crushing blows. One of her children died tragically in an accident, her husband unexpectedly died of a heart attack, and her daughter's new baby was oscillating between life and death. She was so depressed. She told Ethel she had met "Wilma Jones" a few days previously and had started to unburden her heart. Wilma listened for a moment, but only for a moment, and then interrupted to tell how tough a time her cousin had had with her operation and how she herself was suffering with pain in her knee.

Ethel's friend wept and confessed that she had wanted to shout at Wilma there in the street, "Will you shut up about your tiny troubles and let me tell you about my heartache! Will you not keep quiet about your trivial concerns and listen to what's destroying me?"

Wilma not only lacked the sensitivity to listen until this hurting woman was finished, she hadn't the sense to differentiate between the usual and the crushing.

Hang

Nails

and

Colon

Cancers

♦

153

To lament over "sufferings" that are nothing much more than a source of irritation is to run the risk of losing credibility with the world of real sufferers.

To lament over "sufferings" that are nothing much more than a source of irritation is to run the risk of losing credibility with the world of real sufferers. To call on the intercessory work of Christ and the Holy Spirit to relieve us of "troubles" that multiplied millions daily experience but are happily unaware of is to cheapen ourselves and our faith.

"Do not let your hearts be troubled. Trust in God;
trust also in me."

—John 14:1

✦

Can You Still Trust Me?

I don't think it's the crying or the pleading that troubles God—not a bit. The Bible is filled with men and women who, in their pain, turned their eyes heavenward and asked for a break, asked "Why?" Robert Davidson has assured us that "Why?" occurs more often in the Psalms than "Hallelujah!"[1]

A biblical response to suffering only means something to those who give credence to the Bible. Those who will have nothing to do with it will impatiently dismiss it, but that option isn't open to those of us who profess allegiance to Jesus Christ.

Suppose we met Christ, in one of our unhappier moods, when we were hurting sore or were depressed by

SIX:

The God

Who

Allows

Suffering

♦

156

the day-to-day pressures of life, and suppose we hotly demanded that he explain our sufferings and he said, "Sit down and tell me about it."

So we sit down, in pain, fevered and complaining. "My problem's this, you see; I'm having an awful time with my health. My kidneys are failing and I'm diabetic. I'm struggling with infections they can't seem to get rid of . . . And my children; I'm losing my children. They're drifting off into drugs. . . ."

"How do you explain your kidney problems and these terrible infections?" he might ask.

"They're not sure, but there's . . ."

"So, you aren't blaming me for these infections, are you?"

"Well, you could have kept them from me. You could help them to cure me."

"That's true, but what if the whole situation is more complex than you know, and what if I choose not to exempt you from the troubles you are undergoing? Knowing how I feel toward you, can you still trust me?"

"I don't want you to think I don't care for you because I don't grant every request."

"But you've cured other people; you've removed their burdens. At times I think you play favorites and I'm one of those who's left out."

"And have I done nothing for you? I mean, you have friends and food, doctors and medicine, a comfortable home and good neighbors. Don't you think there are millions in the world who would look at you and think you are 'in' and they are the ones who are left out? You've enjoyed years of good health, good food, a fine home, an adequate income, and all these other blessings. You have life with me, a place in the Covenanted Community, and hope for the future. Don't these things count? I don't see how you can feel you've been 'left out' of any good that's going."

And we might ask, "Are you saying I shouldn't ask for help? That I've been blessed more than enough and should just stick it out without bringing my requests to you?"

"No, of course not! I'm just saying I don't want you to think I don't care for you because I don't grant every request. I don't want you to dismiss all that I've done down the years for you and those you love, as if I had done nothing. I don't want you to accuse me of not caring for you because I allow you to undergo what I allow multiplied millions to undergo every day.

"I don't want you saying I left you unblessed. I don't want you to make your allegiance to me hinge on whether I grant all your requests.

"I want you to trust me."

"But you don't understand," we might say, "how the day-after-day pressures weigh a person down and how much they need help to hang on."

"Perhaps I understand more than you know. Maybe you've forgotten who you're speaking to. You can't know how much I want you to trust me."

> *"Everything that is written by the prophets about the Son of Man will be fulfilled. He will be handed over to the Gentiles. They will mock him, insult him, spit on him, flog and kill him."*
>
> —Luke 18:31–32

✦

12
Bad Fridays and "Good Friday"

I remember it clearly. It was in a distant city, and it was the Winders' baby. I was asked to say a few words at the graveside of the little girl. The Winders were heartbroken, of course. The mother insisted on leaving her hospital bed long enough to go to the funeral. Many friends and fellow students had gathered to express their love and share the pain of this pair. People everywhere were weeping openly. The wind was icy; it was bitterly cold. The mourners trembled both with the cold and their shared pain. There lay the casket, there sat the fragmented couple, there were the pained friends, and God couldn't even arrange a fine day for the funeral. It was Friday, April 9, 1982. *Good Friday!*

SIX:

The God

Who

Allows

Suffering

♦

160

I reflected back on another Friday, several years earlier, when my own family stood beside a grave where our grandbaby, Sarah, was to be laid. And I've thought about another Friday, here in Northern Ireland, when I stood by the graveside of my sister-in-law, Elizabeth. It was even colder then; the wind was raw, and the rain was dripping down inside my collar. Our teeth chattered, and our feet froze, and I remember thinking, "What an awful day for a funeral."

Everyone around those graves on those Fridays wanted the loved ones to live, wished they were back, wished they hadn't gone and left us lonely and sad.

But I have read of another gloomy Friday when the grave of a loved one was surrounded by guards *who didn't* want him alive again, who didn't wish him back, who didn't miss him or feel an awful emptiness since he had "gone away," who not only wished him dead, wished him to stay dead, but would kill him again if they had to.

That Friday, a Christian would tell you, was the blackest, most brainless Friday in human history—a Friday when a mindless planet hounded their only Savior to death. If ever there was a bad Friday, that was it; for on that day, in the murder of Jesus of Nazareth, humanity made it clear that it was capable of an Auschwitz, a Gulag prison system, or the brutal torture and murder of any innocent anywhere on this globe. That Friday made it clear that humanity would kill its God if it could lay its hands on him!

How could that Friday compare in horror with so many other days when the death of an innocent didn't come quickly, as it had for the young man from Nazareth. How could the death of one young man rate a second glance in light of the world's horror camps? How could Golgotha compare with Dachau? How could the quick, ruthless murder of the innocent young Galilean bear comparison with the long, drawn-out agonies of those who suffered under Mengele's horrible "experiments" or the death squads of South America?

How could the death of one young man rate a second glance in light of the world's horror camps?

The greater horror, a Christian would tell you, is not in the measure of physical pain. *Of course* many have suffered more in physical terms than the young carpenter. Christians will tell you that the greater horror lies in the person who suffered at Golgotha—this was *God* that we killed. A humanity that is lunatic enough to kill its God and drive him right out of the world is a humanity that will devour its children, pollute its women, and humiliate and torture its men. And because the young man who was dying on the cross outside Jerusalem was the representative of all the innocents of all the ages, Golgotha *was* Buchenwald and Siberia, it was Pol Pot's Cambodia and Papa Doc's Haiti.

But that wicked Friday became "Good Friday." I know that for those whose pain drives them to speechlessness, *the* Story is hard to hear much less believe. That's why it isn't hard to understand the response of Francois Mauriac, 1952 Nobel Prize winner, when he heard Elie Wiesel's horror story of watching the execution of his parents and siblings in a Nazi camp.

> And I, who believe that God is love, what answer could I give my young questioner? . . . Did I speak of that other Jew, his brother . . . the Crucified?

SIX:

The God

Who

Allows

Suffering

. . . Did I affirm that the stumbling block to his faith was the cornerstone of mine? . . . If the Eternal is the Eternal, the last word for each one of us belongs to Him. This is what I should have told this Jewish child. But I could only embrace him, weeping.[1]

◆

*"Go back and report to John what you have seen and heard:
The blind receive sight, the lame walk, those who have
leprosy are cured, the deaf hear, the dead are raised,
and the good news is preached to the poor."*
—Luke 7:22

✦

 # Go Tell John

There have been a lot of strange children born into the world. Not many were stranger than this little boy they called John. He was the child of aged parents, and before his story had hardly begun, he vanished from sight into the wilderness where he grew up. At the critical moment, this man of the wild began preaching a message of repentance and the coming kingdom, and people from the surrounding cities flocked to hear him.

John fearlessly spoke for God and on behalf of the Messiah. He denied he was anyone special, wanted no big fuss made of himself, knew and was pleased to know that he was second fiddle in God's purposes. He defied a king and his wicked consort and was thrown into prison—a

SIX:

The God

Who

Allows

Suffering

◆

164

virtual hole in the ground. This man of the open spaces was suffocating in a pit for the honor of God and the name of the Messiah.

And what report did he hear while he was suffering in prison? He heard stories of miracles and stories of successes wrought by the Messiah. But what of John? Why was he permitted to suffocate in prison, day after day? Two disciples were sent by him to the Messiah with the question, "Are you the one who was to come, or should we expect someone else?"[1]

Had the report been of failures and weakness, we could more easily understand such a question. Why would miracles and power provoke this question? John wasn't looking for information—he was looking for liberation! Poor, brave man, the prison was choking him. Hadn't he stood for God? Hadn't he labored for the Messiah? Had his cousin forgotten this? And so they came in the name of the suffering servant to Jesus, and they put the question.

"At that very time," the text tells us, "Jesus cured many who had diseases, sicknesses and evil spirits, and gave sight to many who were blind." Then he said, "Go [tell] John what you have seen and heard: The blind receive sight, the lame walk, those who have leprosy are cured, the deaf hear, the dead are raised, and the good news is preached to the poor. Blessed is the man who does not fall away on account of me."[2]

"What took you so long?" we can imagine John asking his disciples.

"We gave him your message, but he made us wait while he healed a multitude of people. Master, you should see the power that God has given to him."

"Yes . . . and what did he say?" And they would have told him the words of the Master, about the healings, the raisings, the cleansings, the transformations, and the liberations.

"Did he say anything about getting me out of here?" he might have asked.

"Nothing!" But he did say, "Tell John, blessed is the one who isn't offended at me."

There are few things that test faith more than God changing everything for others and changing nothing for us. To see changed lives and joy-filled faces, to hear wondrous stories of the sun breaking through for other needy people while we are left in our need—*is anything more painful than that?*

And why did Jesus make the two disciples watch while he demonstrated his liberating power? He wanted John to know two things. One, the work of rescue by God was indeed going on, and two, he wanted John to know the reason he would not be rescued—it wasn't because Christ *couldn't* free him; he *wouldn't* free him.

And how did he explain that to this wounded man? This faithful but living-in-agony man? He didn't! He gently said, "John, trust me."

There are few things that test faith more than God changing everything for others and changing nothing for us.

It's too much to ask! He shouldn't have done that! Are we being offended at Jesus? Blessed is the one who doesn't find Jesus a stumbling block. From the text, we can almost feel his eyes moving from those disciples and fixing on us, and we can almost hear him in our seemingly endless pain, gently saying, "Trust me."

Maybe—poor, hurting sufferer—maybe if we knew him better and loved him more, maybe we would need fewer explanations.

They asked Mrs. Einstein if she understood Albert's two theories of relativity. She admitted she didn't, but she said, "You can trust Albert!"

♦

> *"We rejoice in our sufferings, because we know that suffering produces perseverance; perseverance, character; and character, hope. And hope does not disappoint us, because God has poured out his love into our hearts by the Holy Spirit, whom he has given us."*
> —Romans 5:3–5

✦

"What Doesn't Destroy Me Makes Me Strong"

"Just like a Christian," somebody mutters when reading a title like that; "they're so quick to smile through other people's tears." Well, as a matter of fact, it wasn't a Christian who said, "What doesn't destroy me makes me strong." It was the most vehement atheist in modern history, Friedrich Neitzsche.[1] Even this sad but fierce critic of Christians knew that pain could be made to serve.

And where will I go from here? Should I tell you that God gives a child leukemia, a short and agonizingly painful life, just to teach the parents patience or develop their compassion for others? And what are these children to be taught? These children whose time here is so short and so saturated with pain!

SIX:

The God

Who

Allows

Suffering

♦

168

Are children so dispensable as persons that they must endure weeks and months, even years of needles, wires, tubes, nausea, agony, abscesses, chemicals, transfusions, hemorrhages, radiation, questions, machines, curtains—for no other reason than to make some other people somewhat better?

I protest in the name of God! *No!*

But since some children will, in a world of our shaping, a world under judgment because of our wickedness—since some children will go through all this, let us not allow their crucifixions to go for nothing. Let's not permit them to endure all this without learning from them; let their brief and painful visit here brand our pursuit of more—let it brand our self-serving—as the self-centered paganism it is.

Let us allow their awful pain to show us our common humanity, to help us see the pain in the lives of other families, to help us appreciate the struggles of a world where so many weep alone because they believe no one cares. Let their sobs and groans turn our eyes from new cosmetics to new cures, from more "things" for us to more health for them, from the trivializing of life in paltry pursuits to noble living, as we band together in the name of God against the evils nourished by sin and ignored by our selfishness. Let their pain-filled existences remind us of the judgment under which we sit, the debt we owe to God and one another.

Who would deliberately subject their child or other loved one to a daily crucifixion simply to teach a few others ethical uprightness? But I have seen and heard of, and so have you, those who—having done all they could to ease the pain of those they loved and lost—forced that shattering experience to become a servant both to themselves and to other sufferers. This we've seen, not in ones or twos, not in tens or hundreds, but in thousands and tens of thousands. They were made strong and compassionate. They didn't all wither and die under the blows. When pain came forcing its way uninvited into their lives, when they saw it couldn't be resisted, they changed their tactics. Pain would make itself lord, but these brave ones, by God's grace, made it a servant.

"Come on in, then," they said, "you couldn't enter if God did not allow it, and if he allows it, good can come of it!"

One brave sufferer who was enduring a long and painful illness spoke with courage to one of his sympathetic friends and said, "I do not mind that God is driving his ploughshare deep; he purposes a good crop!"

> **Pain would make itself lord, but these brave ones, by God's grace, made it a servant.**

Harry Fosdick became positively angry with people who, as he saw it, tried to reconcile the goodness of God with the horror of suffering. "He doesn't *want* to be reconciled to it," he would hotly protest. "He wants us to band together and hound it out of the world if we can."[2] How true that is!

Don't try to reconcile God with the porn industry, the booze industry, the vice rings, the child prostitution rings, the drug barons, the stinking, crawling, seething tenement buildings that families cower in and pay hard-earned money for. He doesn't want to be reconciled to them! He wants to be known as their enemy. If his will were done, if people paid attention to his desires, none of

SIX:

The God

Who

Allows

Suffering

♦

170

this would exist. He is not at peace with it. When people speak as if he is content with it all, we can almost hear him thunder, *"That's not me; that's not anything like me!"*

The life of Jesus Christ is characterized by Peter as one in which he "went about doing good and healing all that were oppressed by the devil, for God was with him."[3] His life here was one long protest against the pain and suffering in the world, and his healings told what he wanted— not only for those he healed—but for the whole world. That the problem is complex—that what he is ultimately after is humanity reconciled with God and the consequent blessing that would bring—shouldn't fool us into thinking that he shrugs at awful pain. He didn't introduce it into the world—we did! And he wants it removed from the world—we keep it here.

Think noble things of God. If you are God's, you haven't seen the last of your hurting baby—your little boy is safe with him, your little girl is in his loving care—they wait the reunion when all tears will be wiped away. Until then, miss them, but be brave. Until then, shed your tears, but be brave. Until that day rejoice in hope and be strong. Seek out others who hurt as you do but who don't have the hope that is yours in Christ Jesus. Tell them the loss need not be forever. And when someone like you, one who has endured a soul-wrenching loss, puts their arms around a poor bewildered sufferer, not only will that sufferer find some comfort by your being there, you will be strangely helped by the fact that your own suffering has given to you a healing power that countless others know nothing of. You will understand, in your own softened but strengthened heart, "What does not destroy me makes me strong."

✦

The One Who Holds the Knife

If it's no shame to weep at the airport when you're waving a loved one good-bye for six months or a year, why would it be thought shameful to weep as they die because they will be away longer? Christians weep when loved ones die, not because they are without hope, but because, like everybody else, they miss those they love when they go away.

And Christians, in their better moments, don't wish to be exempt from all the pain humanity suffers—it's okay with them that they share the hurts that humans experience—why shouldn't they? Didn't their Lord become incarnate to do just that?

SIX:

The God

Who

Allows

Suffering

♦

172

What Christians have that unbelievers don't is the conviction that pain and death are not the last words or the final realities. Beyond the pain, says the Christian, there is God who wants *life* for us, who allows pain but will not allow it to win, who permits suffering but will not permit it to be lord. Should darkness descend on us, should lightning strike us, should death overtake us, should disease seize us—we are yet safe, for he who is Lord of all has made a commitment to us. We have no fear of anything over which he has control, for he who controls it all loves us.

The husband came home through a violent storm. Lightning shattered the skies and thunder rolled and boomed, winds shrieked, trees creaked and crashed, rain lashed the streets, and it seemed as if the world itself were in torment. She was so glad to see him home safe and held him close for a long time.

"There, there, I'm okay," he said gently.

"Weren't you afraid?" she asked him.

He assured her he hadn't been afraid.

"And how could you not be afraid in such a terrible storm?" she persisted as she made the meal.

He jumped up, took a sharp knife from the drawer and, with a growl, held it close to her throat. She giggled at his silliness.

"Aren't you afraid with this sharp knife so close to your throat?" he hissed, trying to sound sinister and threatening. She laughed.

"The one who holds the knife is my lover," she said. "He would never do me harm."

He slumped back into his chair. "And the Lord of the storm is my Father," he murmured; "he would do me no harm."

How we view the universe makes a difference. Is the universe just a great skull, and when we look into the night sky are we just looking into an empty eye socket? Is there someone there? Is he in control, and does he care? To believe with the British scientist and philosopher Bertrand Russell and some others that eternal, mindless matter is our father and mother, that the universe is our womb and our tomb, that the end of all will come in the complete and absolute death of a universe in ruins, with silent planets and asteroids existing in frozen space and utter blackness[1]—to believe that, to *really* believe that, would be suffering indeed. Such a universe would be mindless and pointless—a universe that cares neither for our coming or our going.

♦

God allows pain but will not allow it to win; he permits suffering but will not permit it to be lord.

Viktor Frankl suffered much in the Nazi torture chambers. In camps where everyone was subjected to so much pain and had so many problems of their own to wrestle with, there wasn't a lot of pity for others. One of the things that helped Frankl beyond measure was the conduct of one of the kitchen detail. This man always served with his eyes fully down so he could see only the plate and not the person. He was maintaining his integrity even in a world of hate and pain. He didn't wish to see the face of a friend in case he gave him extra and cheated another. He didn't wish to see the face of someone he didn't like in case he gave him less and cheated him. Frankl knew that in a universe of savage injustice, he would experience fair treatment from this man. It mattered to someone that people got fair treatment, and if they would get it nowhere else, they'd get it from him as he handed out the food.[2]

And can humans care, even in the awful conditions of a death camp, and the God and Father of Jesus Christ not?

Think noble things of God!

♦

✦

"It Seemed Good in Thy Sight"

A gentleman visited a home for children who could not hear or speak, tells Joseph Parker. The visitor was deeply moved—especially by the silence of the children, which seemed to reflect the silence of their world. He was urged to ask them a question by writing it on the blackboard. This is what he wrote: "Why did God allow you to be deaf and dumb while I have speech and hearing?" Who knows why he chose that question, but he did. For a moment they just looked at each other; it was a mystery no one there could fathom. No one was clever enough to give a wise explanation, but one young man had something better than that—he had trust. He went to the blackboard and wrote, "Even so, Father, for so it seemed good in thy sight."[1]

SIX:

The God

Who

Allows

Suffering

◆

176

But that kind of story only makes the pain of some poor sufferers worse. People today aren't ninteenth-century children locked away in some charity home where they are drilled in piety and faith in God. "It explains nothing," they protest. That's true. It explains nothing; it was the response of a trusting heart.

"But I want to ask him questions. I want to make him explain himself. I want to put him on trial!"

Put *him* on trial? The One on the hill? If we cannot trust him, in light of what he has already said and done, what makes us think we would trust his explanation of our pain and loss, even if he gave one?

Maybe if we had a really satisfying explanation of *his* suffering, our own might take on a different complexion. Maybe if we listened as sympathetically to *his* Story as we want him to listen to ours, we would feel less anxious to put him on trial.

What if he came into your poor, pain-filled life with his own breaking heart? What if he came to you looking for comfort, as he came to other friends one night in a garden? Would you then demand that he explain himself? Or would your heart not—those hearts who have suffered so much, who *are* suffering so much—would your heart not go out to him; and if the occasion required, would you not wrap your arms around him and whisper to him that his pain and loneliness were not for nothing?

And would you not, as he rose to leave, wish him well, encourage him to be brave and believe in God? Yes, you would. And when you remembered that you too are bearing your own share of pain, might you not speak after him: "I was wondering if you might explain why my own heart must be so crushed . . . but never mind, for so it seems right in your eyes." And might you not hear the joyful Master whisper back through the gloom, "Bless you! Be brave, and remember—I will listen."

"Consider it pure joy, my brothers, whenever you face trials of many kinds, because you know that the testing of your faith develops perseverance. Perseverance must finish its work so that you may be mature and complete, not lacking anything."
—James 1:2–4

✦

Don't Go through It Alone

Suffering *can* be redemptive. It can bring into our lives what we later, in saner moments, confess was a blessing that couldn't be measured.

I know this must provoke almost to fury someone who's suffering beyond words, whose torment is more likely understated than exaggerated.

If you're someone like this, I beg you to believe that I have no wish to be glib; and I know that if I were in your place, I would find it more difficult to say such things.

But if I were in your place and you in mine, in my desperation, I would want your words to be true!

It's bad enough that so many of us live without health, but worse if we live without purpose or hope! I wouldn't

SIX:

The God

Who

Allows

Suffering

♦

178

want to believe that suffering and death had the last word, that they were the grim ultimates! I would want to believe that these cursed realities could be made to serve some lovely purpose, that I wouldn't have to look at my suffering loved ones or my gangrenous body and shrug helplessly without hope!

When we say suffering and death can be redemptive, we're not saying they're not hateful or excruciating; we're not saying the sufferers aren't in agony. No! We're speaking our faith that God will not allow us to face *anything* without the privilege of his working it for good—if we will but say yes to his offer. He will not allow suffering to be meaningless but will, with our permission, force it to be the soil out of which things like compassion, sympathy, courage, and service grow.

Thousands of people down the years have lived utterly selfish lives until personal tragedy shook their self-centered world or until the torment and need of other sufferers broke the spell that held them captive and freed them to live transformed lives.

> Tell him how painful it is and how you wish you didn't have to go through it, and hear him assure you that you don't have to go through it alone.

In 1859, young Henri Dunant was horrified by the carnage of war at the battle of Solferino in Italy. Then he became enraged and screamed, "Why doesn't God do something about this?" And God did—Dunant organized Red Cross International.

God did not send suffering into our world, but he did send the message of the Hebrew-Christian Scriptures—a message that culminates in Jesus Christ and makes us able to face suffering and death with courage and hope. We don't need to shrug in tearful helplessness or rage in impotence.

What can be honorably removed should be; what can't be cured must be honorably and hopefully endured.

Arthur Gossip was a chaplin during Word War I and knew what it was like to see young men die the horrible deaths of war. "Isn't it enough that you lose them; must you turn away from Him in your pain and lose Him as well? Have you not lost enough?"[1] Turn to him and let him embrace you in his big, strong, loving arms; and do all your crying there. Tell him how painful it is and how you wish you didn't have to go through it, and hear him assure you that you don't have to go through it alone, that he won't let you go through it alone.

✦

The Pain God Bears

It isn't news that when Jesus saw multitudes of sick and sorrowful people, he saw them as sheep without a shepherd and had compassion on them. Somebody exaggerated—but did it nicely—when he said that Jesus virtually banished disease from Palestine during his personal ministry. It hurt Jesus to see people in misery, and it made him angry when people cared little about the suffering of others.

You remember the case of the woman who had been bent double for eighteen long years. When Christ healed her on the Sabbath, a Jewish leader criticized both Jesus and the woman. The synagogue leader was only stating the common view that since she wasn't in danger of

SIX:

The God

Who

Allows

Suffering

♦

182

dying, she could and should have waited until the Sabbath was past before seeking or receiving healing. The infuriated Christ called such people "hypocrites" and told them the poor woman had waited long enough.[1]

Not only did Jesus go around easing the burdens of people, he insisted that a central issue in our judgment will be how we respond to the needs of the hurting.[2]

So anyone who tells us that God cares nothing about the illness and suffering of our world has missed the mark a long way.

Nevertheless, physical comfort is not the bottom line with God. Good health, financial stability, and the other blessings that are part of the social structure he would wish for us in a transformed world are not the big issues with God. It hurts him to see us in real pain, but there is something that hurts him more. Read carefully these words from G. A. Smith. Then read them again to grasp their full meaning.

> The pain which disease and death thus cause to love is nothing to the agony that Sin inflicts when he takes the game into his unclean hands. We know what pain love brings, if our love be a fair face and a fresh body in which Death brands his sores while we stand by, as if with arms bound. But what if our love be a childlike heart, and a frank expression and honest eyes, and a clean and clever mind. Our powerlessness is just as great and infinitely more tormented when Sin comes by and casts his shadow over these. Ah, that is Love's greatest torment when her children, who have run from her to the bosom of sin, look back and their eyes are changed! *That* is the greatest torment of Love—to pour herself without avail into one of those careless natures

which seem capacious and receptive, yet never fill with love, for there is a crack and a leak at the bottom of them. The fields where Love suffers her sorest defeats are not the sick-bed and not death's margin, not the cold lips and sealed eyes kissed without response; but the changed eyes of children . . . and the home the first time the unclean laugh breaks across it. To watch though unable to soothe, a dear body racked with pain, is peace beside the awful vigil of watching a soul shrink and blacken with vice, and your love unable to redeem it.[3]

The Pain

God

Bears

Broken-hearted parents know exactly what Smith means by all this. But if they know it, if they feel such pain and loss, how much more does he feel it who made us all and made us to feel such pain at such a loss? In feeling the agony of such a loss, we've only learned from him, we've only shared to a limited degree the pain he feels without measure.

Physical comfort is not the bottom line with God.

We mustn't allow ourselves to believe that physical suffering and death are the ultimate horrors, and we mustn't see God as above and beyond pain and hurt.

"Endure hardship with us like a good soldier of Christ Jesus."

—2 Timothy 2:3

✦

The Man in the Iron Mask

Like all monarchs in those days, said Alexandre Dumas, Louis XIII was anxious to have a male heir. Imagine his joy when his wife, Anne of Austria delivered a boy child. The child was soon christened, a service of thanksgiving was conducted, and a grand dinner of celebration followed.

Imagine his horror, when a few hours later a discreet and trusted servant whispered the news in his ear that the queen had delivered another son! "One prince is peace and safety for the state; two competitors are civil war and anarchy," was the established view. The firstborn became Louis XIV, and the younger child was sent away.[1]

SIX:

The God

Who

Allows

Suffering

♦

186

The wastrel King Louis was increasingly hated by the subjects of the land, and the existence of his brother was seen by his cronies as a serious threat to the throne and their power base. And so, in the screen adaptation of Dumas' novel, the king's brother, played by Richard Chamberlain, now fully grown but completely unaware of his royal identity, is taken to an island prison. An iron mask is made for the prisoner, and he is never allowed to speak to anyone, not even his jailers. The metal mask brings to perfection the prisoner's sense of isolation, but what drives him to distraction, what leaves him speechless with grief beyond the silence and the suffocation is the *mystery*. As his captors row away, back to the mainland, the sufferer climbs to the window and calls after them, the poignant question, "Why? Why?" But his only answer is the echo of his own words as they reverberate through the still air.

If only he knew why he was being punished. He could argue his case. If he had done something to deserve it, well, then, it would make it easier to bear—but what had he done? "Just tell me *why*," he begs.[2]

Maybe we're asking the wrong questions.

"Make sense of it!" That's what we want from those who come to comfort us. "Show me why it had to be this way."

But maybe we're asking the wrong questions. I know this is a hard saying, and I don't wish to brutalize into silence those who are racked with pain—their own or that of a loved one—but maybe it isn't helpful to ask that our comforters "make sense of it." While the world is under God's control and while he will bring it to a satisfying conclusion, it's still a world where things happen that in and of themselves make no sense. No one designed them to happen. No one planned for the dog to tear the life out of the child. No one planned the wrinkle in the rug that caused the trip that caused the scalding water to pour over the child who's now scarred for life.

"How can we respond to this?" is a better question. "What can we make out of this?" is a braver and more fruitful question. What has happened may not have been anyone's active will (least of all God's—even though he allowed it), but can it be made to serve God, ourselves, and other people?

"Why does it *have* to be this way?" is another question that's understandable under painful circumstances, but maybe it's the wrong question. There isn't a reason in the world to believe the little girl *had* to be born with Down's syndrome—but she was!

Maybe it didn't *have* to be this way, but it *is* this way. The question now is, "How will we respond to it?"

And the God who spared not his own Son watches and waits.

> *"Can a mother forget the baby at her breast and have no compassion on the child she has borne? Though she may forget, I will not forget you!"*
> —Isaiah 49:15

✦

The Beliefs of Unbelief

"If an all-powerful God loves us, why is there so much pain, so much *needless* pain?" This is the question that creates the "problem" of suffering in the Christian faith.

Atheists have no such problem. They don't need to make "sense" out of suffering, for a mindless universe neither knows nor cares about our coming or going. Our situation is without remedy and without purpose; we just happened to appear here, and we'll just happen to disappear when the whole universe grinds to a freezing halt in total blackness and silence. In the view of the atheist, Jean Paul Sartre, existence is a sick joke. The mindless, mechanical universe unconsciously brought consciousness, bringing beings into existence, and will unconsciously and mechanically drive them back again into oblivion.[1]

SIX:

The God

Who

Allows

Suffering

♦

190

We are bacteria that have appeared by chance on the surface of a second-rate planet in an off-the-beaten-track solar system. There is no explaining needed because there is no god—no one who cares, no one with whom you can argue, no one to curse, no one to rebel against or plead with. No one brought you here; you're not here *for* anything; you're not *going* anywhere—except into the oblivion you came out of.

The atheist H. J. Blackham, talking about the atheistic view of our existence, said the greatest objection to it is, "the pointlessness of it all . . . it's too bad to be true."[2] And T. H. Huxley, no friend of Christianity, confessed that his own views appalled him. He was born in 1825 and confessed that as he grew older, the approach of death depressed him more and more. He mourned the fact that with the appearance of 1900 he would be as nonexistent as he had been in 1800. It was the thought of nonexistence that led him to say, "I'd rather be in hell."

The atheist doesn't need to make "sense" out of suffering, for a mindless universe neither knows nor cares about our coming or going.

The beliefs of unbelief may erase the incongruity some see between a loving God and a pain-filled world, but as for me, I much prefer to trust the word of Christ Jesus who knows about suffering and death and questions. I choose to believe his message: "I was alive, became dead, and look—I'm now alive forever. Trust me. Death is overrated, and suffering doesn't mean my Father is weak or loveless."

✦

Tractor-Driving, Cow-Scratching John

Joseph Bayly, a compassionate author and sufferer, got a letter from a woman. Here's what it said:

> On January 25th, 1973, in Memorial Hospital, John Risso, red-haired, laughing, tall, eighteen, tractor-driving, cow-scratching, flirtatious, shy, died after two and a half years of leukemia. After six weeks of a raging temperature, experimental drugs, bleeding, and an abscess in his rectum that became gangrenous, he died soft and gentle, finally, after six hours of violent death throes. His face so thin, his hair only a memory, a soft red fuzz, arms blue and green from shots

SIX:

The God

Who

Allows

Suffering

◆

192

and intravenous feeding, he looked like an old picture of a saint after his tortures were over. . . .

Why would a kind God do what was done to John, or do such a thing to me? I'm poor, have only secondhand furniture and clothing. The things of value were my husband and sons. . . . How can I live with the agony he suffered? . . . Part of the time he was in a coma, and he kept saying, "Mama, help me, Mama, help me." I couldn't and it's killing me. I whispered in his ear, "John, I love you so much." All of a sudden his arm came up stiffly and fell across my back, and very quietly he said, from some vast depth, "Me too."[1]

Read the letter again and note the gracious and tender tone of this woman, even in the midst of her heartbreak. What we read isn't bitterness poured out but anguish spoken—anguish, not looking for information, anguish looking for some way to tell of a loss so profound that it must be uttered—somebody must hear it. It grows out of a love that cannot leave John's story untold.

Maybe, John, the powerful love of your mother explains *your* strength and tenderness. Your "Me too!" spoken by a young boy in the middle of awful, awful torment, fills us with feelings of love and admiration for you. You fill us with hope that maybe we, too, in the middle of our torment or final goodbye can speak the words that others long to hear.

In dying as you did, you have made me want to be brave, not only at the moment of my death, but while I live. The effort, emotionally and physically, to respond to your mother's whispered love, that arm rising stiffly and falling across her back, the "me too" from some vast depth, will stay with me all my life, affecting me even when I'm not conscious of it. Thank you.

> *"By his death he might destroy him who holds the power of death—that is, the devil—and free those who all their lives were held in slavery by their fear of death."*
>
> —Hebrews 2:14–15

✦

"Sent to Me by Heaven"

In prison, waiting to be transported to the killing center, an innocent girl prepares to die. Condemned to die for plotting against the Republic with Charles Darnay, the love of her life, she asks him to hold her hand during the ordeal—because, she said, while she wasn't afraid of dying, she was a little weak. The unseen man next to her, assures her that he will do that until the very end. Upon hearing his voice, she realizes with astonishment that this is not Darnay and that a stranger is dying in Darnay's place. Sydney Carton, a dissolute lawyer, had fallen in love with the lovely, young Lucie. Though she didn't return his love, his love for her was power enough to bring him to his place in this rumbling cart headed for

SIX:

The God

Who

Allows

Suffering

♦

194

the guillotine—a willing substitute for Charles Darnay. He gently hushes her words and gives her the assurance she asked for. His company, his loving heart, and his calm approach to death make all the difference to her. As they rumble to that place, her hand in his, she says, "But for you, dear stranger, I should not be so composed, for I am naturally a poor little thing, faint of heart; nor should I have been able to raise my thoughts to Him who was put to death, that we might have hope and comfort here today. I think you were sent to me by Heaven."[1]

While the New Testament emphasis, without question, is on the *atoning* nature of Christ's death, it also promises that his death has the power to free us from the *fear* of our own deaths: "Since the children have flesh and blood, he too shared in their humanity so that by his death he might destroy him who holds the power of death—that is, the devil—and free those who all their lives were held in slavery by their fear of death."[2] His death frees us from the *fear* of death.

Bunyan, in *Pilgrim's Progress,* tells us that Christian and Hopeful are near the end of their journey to the Celestial City but have yet to cross a river, deep and mysterious, if they are to enter the city. The sight of it worries Christian, but since there was no alternative, he and Hopeful enter. Christian begins to sink and calls out to his friend, "I sink in deep waters; the billows go over my head, all the waves go over me." Hopeful calls back, "Be of good cheer, my brother, I feel the bottom, and it is sound."

Despite our fear, there is nothing to fear. Death is no bottomless pit; there is a bottom to it, and it is sound. As we rumble toward our meeting with death, the Christ comes to our side, and when we ask him, "Why are you here?" he tells us, "I was sent to you by Heaven. Keep your eyes on me and mind no other object."

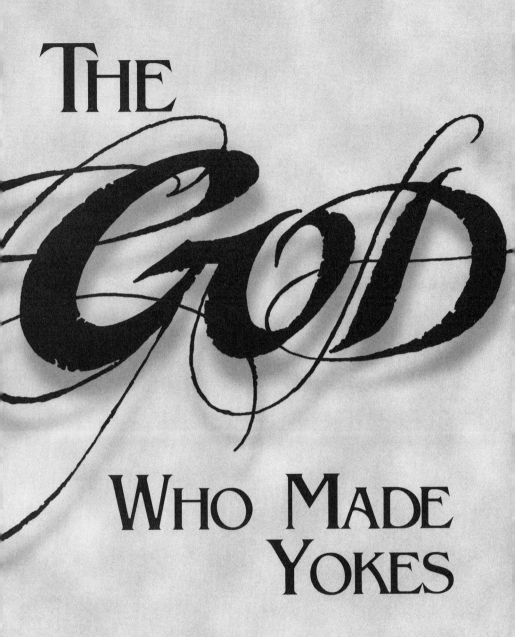

THE God

WHO MADE YOKES

· SEVEN ·

> *"He had no beauty or majesty to attract us to him, nothing in his appearance that we should desire him."*
>
> —Isaiah 53:2

✦

Not What They Expected

It's easier than it used to be, but I still have difficulty seeing God knee-deep in wood shavings. I'd have the same difficulty if he had come as a grease-covered auto mechanic or a well-dressed bank clerk. I have some difficulty seeing him as anything but a world-beating teacher and preacher of Scripture. To see him as someone who day after day carved on yokes for oxen or tables or doorposts is a challenge.

First-century fathers were expected to teach their children a trade, so Joseph undoubtedly taught Jesus about carpentry. Reflect a while on him going to the shop and putting in the hours, day after day—carefully measuring, smoothing, and shaping. Yes, but what about stilling

SEVEN:

The God

Who

Made

Yokes

♦

198

storms? What about ridding Palestine of disease and suffering? What about the proclamation of the saving message the country and the world needed to hear? Must these glorious things wait while God makes tables and benches and ox yokes? Is it not an awful comedown for the hands that shaped the planets and formed the galaxies to make tools for peasant farmers? That God is the God of the extraordinary we all know full well, but it's just as true that he has an intimate attachment to the "ordinary."

The only God we know, the only true and living God, chose to reveal himself in a peculiar way, in a strand of history recorded for us in the Hebrew-Christian Scriptures. He worked with men and women from "Main Street," as well as kings and queens from plush palaces.

Listen to how the prophet Isaiah described him: "He grew up before him like a tender shoot, and like a root out of dry ground. He had no beauty or majesty to attract us to him."[1] Why, he looked just like the rest of us. He was so ordinary that some who met him saw absolutely nothing in him that was extraordinary.

Is this not an awful comedown for the hands that shaped the planets and formed the galaxies to make tools for peasant farmers?

Years ago I watched the movie *"Oh, God!"* Despite the obvious trash in it, I learned some lessons I'll never forget. A supermarket manager gets a letter from God granting him an interview he never asked for. Eventually he goes to the address given, the twenty-seventh floor (I think) of a seventeen-floor building. In the room is a chair and a voice. The manager, believing it to be a hoax, demands that "God" show himself. "God" assures him that if he showed himself as he was, the results would be disastrous for the manager. Eventually, "God" decides to reveal himself to the manager, and when he does, we see a little man wearing baggy pants, tennis shoes, a checkered shirt, a wind-breaker, a golfing cap, and thick glasses. The manager stares in utter disbelief!

"Well? What did you expect?" the little man asks.

At first I was amused, then offended, and finally instructed. I'd just seen, in an updated version, what the gospel of Mark says about Jesus:

◆

> And many who heard him were amazed. "Where did this man get these things?" they asked. "What's this wisdom that has been given him, that he even does miracles! Isn't this the carpenter? Isn't this Mary's son and the brother of James, Joseph, Judas and Simon? Aren't his sisters here with us?" And they took offense at him.[2]

He wasn't what they expected.

When the fiery John the Baptist informed the multitudes that there was one among them so amazing that even untying the thongs of his sandals was a task too lofty for John,[3] perhaps they looked around themselves for this noble figure. And did their eyes fall, as J. G. Greenhough suggests, on the carpenter from Nazareth and then move on in search of a more likely person?[4] Had they seen him, wouldn't they have classed him immediately as a village tradesman, labeled him "ordinary," and dismissed him? He wasn't what they expected.

"And if anyone gives even a cup of cold water to one of these little ones because he is my disciple, I tell you the truth, he will certainly not lose his reward."

—Matthew 10:42

✦

The Glory of the Ordinary

We live in a world that worships the grand, the great, the outstanding. Our task is to see the glory in the ordinary.

We tend to be disappointed if we are classed as "Mr. or Ms. Average." We'd rather be up there among the record-breakers, the indispensables—even if we know in our bones we aren't one of the "gifted" ones. Again and again I hear people saying they would like to serve God in a *significant* way. There's nothing wrong with the words; they may even be noble. I'm just saying that too much is made of "winners" as distinct from the "rank and file."

It isn't enough, it would seem, to be glowing with love for Christ and permeating society for him, like leaven. The world is thought to belong to the endless grinners,

SEVEN:

The God

Who

Made

Yokes

♦

202

the smile-flashing evangelists with their back-slapping ways, and the super-duper youth ministers whose feet rarely touch the ground. The victorious people are those who'll "Hallelujah!" at the drop of a hat or "Praise the Lord!" at the most commonplace remark. The rest are "living in the wilderness"; the rest haven't gotten out of Romans 7 and into Romans 8. Poor devils.

I talked to a young man some time ago about the suffering to which we've been called. I won't soon forget his openly irritated response. "Where's all the victory and triumph in Christ then?" Posters with people on them who look like they've just experienced a major tragedy are often tacked on the walls of our buildings. The caption asks something like, "Is this how a Christian should look?" Not only is this no way to produce smiles (which I presume is what the posters are supposed to do), it ignores a large slice of life. Sometimes I think these blessed, smiling ones would have rebuked the Master in Gethsemane with, "Smile, God loves you!"

We live in a world that worships the grand, the great, the outstanding. Our task is to see the glory in the ordinary.

Christ's years as a carpenter were "ordinary." He displayed no fevered fanaticism, no hysteria. Yet he joyfully and worshipfully fitted a handle, smoothed a corner, and drove a nail until he heard the whispers coming up from the Judean desert, laid down his joinery tools, and hit the road. And even then, he became no ranting hack who pounded assemblies into furious attempts to keep up with the population explosion. He knew all about the dying millions, but that didn't keep him from being calm in his soul as he went about fulfilling with joyful seriousness the will of God for his life.

Who gains if I urge people to do less for God? No one! Not God, not me, not anyone else. That's not my aim. I'm wanting to say something about the "ordinary" that will encourage the ordinary to live radiantly and vibrantly in their "ordinariness." I'm for gifted evangelists and authors, but I'm just as thrilled at the loving embrace of a mother when she makes her fourteen-year-old boy know, by a warm upbringing, that Christ is indeed alive and caring for him through his mother. I'll take that anytime over the three- or five-year sprint of some fired-up evangelist or youth minister.

Radio preacher Daniel Poling told of the death of an outstanding author, conference teacher, and social leader—a lady lauded and applauded. Her son was a well-known and respected citizen in the town. Everyone was at the funeral to hear her son say, as he stood by the coffin, "I don't remember you for your books or your well-earned reputation. I remember you as one with a warm and loving embrace, whose lips pressed on mine in days of doubt, uncertainty and when I needed acceptance. I remember you as my mother."[1] There are a few outstanding authors (for which we should fervently thank God!), but there are millions of ordinary mothers and fathers and friends who shape the world generation after generation (and often produce world-beating preachers and writers).

Thomas Paine, the eighteenth-century deist, is quoted as saying to some believers, "I think I can answer all your arguments, but I can't begin to answer the holy and loving life of my mother."

SEVEN:

The God

Who

Made

Yokes

♦

204

What raises ordinariness above "ordinariness" is dedicating what we are and have to the name of God and living for him in faithfulness and gladness. If you're involved with Christ in this way, worry about *nothing*. If you feel you aren't able to be involved in any of the assembly's special programs, don't worry about it. Carry out the "program" you *know* God has laid before you and consider the rest.

There are few outstanding authors, but there are millions of ordinary mothers and fathers and friends who shape the world generation after generation.

Refuse to be intimidated into thinking that the ordinary is only a little more useful than useless. Raise your children well; be a loyal and noble friend. Thank God genuinely for the vim and verve of the fast-moving evangelists and leaders who dream lovely dreams—dreams that are only brought to reality by the masses of the ordinary people. For at least eighteen years of his short life here, the Master contented himself with the ordinary.

> *"Whatever you do, work at it with all your heart, as working for the Lord. . . . You will receive an inheritance from the Lord as a reward. It is the Lord Christ you are serving."*
>
> —Colossians 3:23–24

✦

The Sacredness of the Secular

The years between twelve and thirty could be called the years of "inglorious service" in contrast to the years of Christ's public ministry, but that would be an awful mistake. The fact that he spent those years in what Christians are prone to call "secular work" makes it clear that he rejects the way we dichotomize life.

By "secular" we usually mean it has no "religious" content, that it isn't immediately related to holiness or spirituality. Preaching, for example, is "sacred," and cabdriving is "secular." One handles sacred things, and the other just drives a hack. A woman is a bank officer and a Sunday school teacher. The first position is secular and the

SEVEN:

The God

Who

Made

Yokes

♦

206

second is sacred. We promote uneasiness in one person by telling him his work has no spiritual root and superiority in the other by assuring her that only her work ("church work") really counts. This isn't biblical!

We mean well when we say, "He makes a living being an engineer, but he really works for the Lord as a soul-winner." I don't think the God who made yokes would accept such a distinction. Paul called the Ephesians to work to provide for the needy. He regarded providing for one's family a sacred obligation and went so far as to call a man an infidel who wouldn't do it.[1] Of course there's such a thing as "secular," but if what we do can be and is devoted to God, it isn't secular—it's sacred!

God with a saw in his hand buries forever our "this is secular and that is sacred" notions and explodes our view that the physical is worldly. But he does something much more wonderful than that; he gives us, by his own example, the message that earthly affairs are holy! Well, more accurately, he gives us the message that earthly affairs can be invested with holiness.

Jesus gives us the message that earthly affairs can be invested with holiness.

Jesus never involved himself in anything that wasn't pleasing to his Father, and in obedience to his Father's will, he worked as a carpenter. The activity was lawful and offered to God out of a pure heart. Jesus didn't spend those years "marking time" until he "really" got to work for God as a speaker. No one ever brought a piece of shoddy work back to Jesus, because he didn't work just for people; he worked for his Father by working for people. And once we can see him as a carpenter, it isn't hard to imagine him stepping back from a finished bench and glancing toward heaven with a "How does that look to you?"

Many categorize being a waiter or waitress as a "secular" job, but in Acts 6 when they wanted men to "wait on tables," they chose men who were full of faith and the Holy Spirit.[2] Organizing and setting down food for people wasn't secular to them—they thought it was sacred.

It isn't what one is doing that determines the secularity or sacredness of it—it's the purpose and intent. The preacher rises and delivers a mighty message from Scripture. Sacred? Maybe! If he has done it to the glory of God. Paul spoke of those who "huckstered" the Word of God. To teach the Scriptures to one's own advantage is unholy pandering, and there are those who minister the Word out of envy.[3]

There's no doubt that motive enters into the cabdriver's case. If his aim is mere personal aggrandizement (I can hear some cabdrivers jeering at that!) or the pursuit of luxury without regard for God, why, then, he's no more holy than the self-exalting preacher. He is secular to the core. The rich fool worked hard; was he not entitled to lay up goods for himself? But Christ pronounced him covetous—even of his own goods. He was not rich toward God;[4] and if I understand the thrust of this text, he was not rich toward his neighbor either.

Here's how Paul addressed some disciples in Colossae: "Slaves, obey your earthly masters in everything; and do it, not only when their eye is on you and to win their favor, but with sincerity of heart and reverence for the Lord. Whatever you do, work at it with all your heart, as working for the Lord, not for men. . . . It is the Lord Christ you are serving."[5]

A job is sacred or secular depending on the heart.

∞

A job isn't secular because you do it with your hands. A minister isn't holy because he ministers in holy things. A job is sacred or secular depending on the heart. *(Of course* it has to be an honorable job!) If my work has no vertical connection, it is secular. We invest our jobs with holiness just as Jesus did his carpentry and preaching.

◆

Stolen Joy

To deny the glory of the ordinary has the effect of
making people discontent and restless. It takes the joy out
of living. Some ministers of the Word cheat those they
teach—actually steal their joy—by permitting them (and
often urging them) to believe that the bulk of their lives
must be shackled to the "secular," while the "ministers"
involve themselves in "the work of God." This is a great
injustice. I wonder how these ministers would have
addressed Jesus as he spent (what?) eight to ten hours
daily in his shop or Paul who sat for hours making tents
to provide for his and others' needs?

I'm not saying disciples should never verbalize for
Christ. I'm not saying that disciples should do nothing

209

SEVEN:

The God

Who

Made

Yokes

♦

210

more than "hold down a job." Thriving and joyous Christians will want and will find ways to share with others their faith in Jesus Christ who loves them. But they won't become thriving and joyous if ministers keep telling them that their "secular" work doesn't count as service to God. I've never met anyone in all my life—never—who wore the name of Christ and felt that his or her only responsibility to God was to "hold down a job." *But I've met hundreds of people who were never told they could offer their daily jobs to God as a holy offering!*

"Nonchurch" workers spend at least one-third of their lives doing what some ministers say has no religious content. And, what's more, it's the third in which they are most alert, most energetic, vibrant, and capable. You know what I mean. All of us are at our best physically, mentally, and emotionally from, say, eight in the morning until six in the evening, and that's when most people are in their "secular" work. How can anyone say that none of that counts!

When they ask what you are doing for Christ and his purpose, ask them if living with integrity under difficult circumstances counts.

When sensitive souls are told that their "secular" work is of no value, they become restless and discontent. They lose the joy they used to find in working unto God (if they ever had any), and they become poor manifestations of joy in Christ. Their religion becomes a dead heave from day to day. Their fellow workers take note and see that the doctrine of Christ is not being adorned and made attractive. The disciples begin to talk of their work as a hindrance to the "real" work they ought to be doing. They begin to believe the preaching and think they are only working for an earthly employer (which is contrary to the explicit words of God).

Larry Peabody's book *Secular Work Is Full-Time Service* speaks of such a person as one who has "lost all zest for the job at hand. There are seldom sufficient hours in the day for such a man. He lives under the anxiety of never being able to do enough for God because so much of his best time is deemed spiritually nonproductive. His view of his work leaves him torn." So after work, he's on the go to "get some hours in for God." Very often family relationships suffer. If he's too tired to get out after work "and [work] for God for a change," he becomes sensitive about the sermons he hears on "doing." Self-recrimination becomes an everyday thing, and a strain develops between him and the leadership "who want [him] to be more involved in the 'work of the Lord.'"[1]

All this sometimes leads Christians to collar non-Christians at work to preach to them. The approach, because it usually must be brief, is often abrasive and pushy rather than invitational. It's often more "glare than share."[2] I've met some who prize the thunder-at-the-door approach, who would buffalo vulnerable Christians into thinking that any other approach is because they "lack the boldness of the Lord." If they can't use a strong approach because it embarrasses them, they sink into a "guilty silence."[3]

Have you never wondered why God has the bulk of all his people in the places of "secular" work? And why he has called so few as evangelists.[4] Most of the people (children of Christian families excluded) who are reached for

SEVEN:

The God

Who

Made

Yokes

♦

212

God rarely come to our assemblies; they're saved by friends and workmates.

Think about it: Most of the people *you* work with don't go to church, so they can't hear the preacher speak of integrity, honesty, cheerfulness, loyalty, helpfulness, contentment—all in the name of Christ. But they can hear it in you, right there on the job where you spend eight hours a day with them. Maybe if you make it attractive, they will be drawn and your opportunity will arise because by God's grace you've created a "redemptive context" in which the Word will have full sway. Don't get ulcers trying to work up the nerve to force a showdown. For those hours each day your *assignment is the marketplace*—"out there" where the non-Christians are—getting to know them in ways you'd never get to know them otherwise, even if they came to our assemblies once a week.

So when the zealous thunderballs among us come ripping through the place with arms and sparks flying, with dreams and schemes pouring from their hot lips, thank God for them, pray for them, and keep your cool. Envy not the zealous their zeal. Do your level best not to be irritated with the (understandable but frequent) overstatements you will hear from such people who are so excited about Christ. And when they ask what you are doing for Christ and his purpose, ask them if praying for the lost counts. Ask them if living with integrity under difficult circumstances counts. Ask them if giving liberally from limited means to support fireball ministers counts. Ask them if suffering bravely or living with holiness in a marriage union or raising children in God's image—ask if any of that counts.

THE GOD

WHO CALLS DISCIPLES

+ EIGHT +

✦

Called to Copy God

The God who is holy, the God who forgives sins and loves the weak, the God of the towel, this God calls us—his disciples—to copy him. This final chapter is by no means meant to be a comprehensive survey of the disciple's call but will focus on just a few of the implications of what we have learned about the God of the Towel.

First and foremost, we must know that the disciple's model is nothing less than God himself. The Phillips translation of Ephesians 5:1 says this, "As children copy their fathers you, as God's children, are to copy him."

Is the disciple called to forgive sinners? We are called to forgive "just as in Christ God forgave you."[1] Are disciples called to accept one another as fellow saints? We are

215

EIGHT:

The God

Who

Calls

Disciples

♦

216

to accept one another "just as Christ accepted you."[2] Are disciples called to esteem one another mutually and think of the needs of others? We are to do it in the mind of Christ whose attitude led him to empty himself for the sake of others.[3] Are disciples called to put away sin and put on righteousness? We are to do so because we have died and been raised with Christ.[4]

And if disciples are to be holy, we are to be holy "as obedient children." "Just as he who called you is holy, so be holy in all you do."[5] The call to holiness is, and has always been, based on God's character and prior attitude toward us. Israel's redemption from Egypt and their creation as a nation unto God was not due to their goodness or national attractiveness—it was due to God's holy nature.[6]

We are not to treat others as we would want others to treat us; we are to treat others as God has already treated us in Jesus Christ.

Christ did not intend the "Golden Rule" to be the ultimate expression of his call to a lovely life. We are not to treat others as we would want others to treat us; we are to treat others as God has already treated us in Jesus Christ. The Israelites kept the covenant in a grateful and loving response to God for what he had *already* done for them. They loved him because he *first* loved them. They were to treat one another the way God had *already* treated them. We are to be and behave as God has already been and behaved toward us in Christ. That and nothing less is God's call to us and God's model for us.

"So then, each of us will give an account of himself to God."

—Romans 14:12

✦

Called to Maturity

Maturity in Christ leads people to upright and loving behavior, but for a person's behavior to be upright and loving, two things must be true: first, it must be done for Christ's sake, and second, it must be done from that *person's* heart and not yours.

You can bully people to their knees, but you can't make them pray. You can coerce them into parting with their money, but you can't force them into the grace of giving. You can emotionally intimidate people into reading the Bible, but you can't thumbscrew them into the loving appreciation of truth. You can browbeat them into using words about Christ and religious convictions, but you can't buffalo them into joyously verbalizing about the

EIGHT:

The God

Who

Calls

Disciples

♦

218

Master they love and wish to love more. You can say what you like, but there's a difference between a heart response to a noble challenge and a person who conforms for fear of being looked down on or ostracized.

Mature behavior has the full support of my inner world. It is behavior not foreign to me. I don't do it just because you want me to. It's behavior *I* choose from within—even if I'm a bit timid about putting it into practice. It isn't something I'm "putting on" simply because you would have me do it. It is behavior that expresses my inner condition *as distinct from* what I do to gain your favor.

It's okay for children to do what their parents want them to do, even if their own hearts don't approve. That has it's own grandeur. It's okay for me to receive guidance from others in areas of ignorance or timidity, but the operative word is *receive.* I want it; it hasn't been forced on me. In fact, confessing limitations and asking for help and guidance can be a sign of maturity.

Maturity involves more than orthodox or approved conduct—it must be *mine!*

I stand my little girl before me. I tell her to make her own decision in choosing between two gifts I'm offering her. "This one is really the best," I say, pointing to A. "Go ahead, make your choice." She looks for a while and makes for B. I stop her and say, "Look, A is really much better than B." She thinks some more and goes for B. I stop her again (I can't understand this kid). "Look, I've told you that A is better than B. How often do I have to tell you. Now make your choice." She looks at me a while and then slowly chooses A. "Attagirl," I tell her. "I'm glad you chose the best." But I notice as she walks off that she isn't as buoyant about the gift as I thought she would be. Ah, well, gratitude is a scarce commodity.

The child *conformed;* she didn't *choose.* I knew what was best for her, so I took away her freedom to choose. I offered her three gifts— A, B and choice—and reneged on the most important one!

We urge believers to pursue their own commitment to Christ; but not content to lay before them possibilities, we proceed to make numerous decisions for them. If they happen to protest, we think them rebels or ungrateful.

People who dominate us in this fashion aren't completely to blame, for *we* put up with it—even encourage it. The charismatic leader is too much for us. He bowls us over, overwhelms us with *his* choice and we fall into line. Of course, in matters of clear-cut good or evil, we all have a right to speak decisively. But the problems lie in the areas of judgment, advice, counsel, and precisely how a mature Christian would act.

Maturity involves more than orthodox or approved conduct—the choice must be *mine!* If what I do or say is to be an expression of my maturity, it must *live out* what is mine *within.*

To correctly formulate the "proofs" given for a particular doctrinal position without an inner approval of it is no mark of maturity. The child repeats words and sounds after us without understanding what they mean, without personal appropriation of them. That's fine for a child; but maturity rejects rote repetition as the child grows into an adult. The early math student repeats the formulas, like a parrot, without a real appreciation of them; but when the student blossoms into a Whitehead, Russell, or Einstein, he leaves mere memorization behind.

EIGHT:

The God

Who

Calls

Disciples

♦

220

It's all right to be ignorant, you understand; it's all right to be immature. But we learn to recognize our condition, and we look for growth. Growth is more than answers, more than approved conduct. It is the ability to weigh advice, knowing how to say "no" in a good way, when others are wanting you to say "yes." It isn't wrong to "go along." Sometimes to "go along" is a mark of maturity—to forfeit rights, to sink your own view (which you think is better, clearer)—these may be marks of real maturity. But to live on someone else's convictions, to be carried along without being fully persuaded in your own mind is something else.

> *"Confess your sins to each other and pray for each other*
> *so that you may be healed."*
>
> —James 5:16

✦

Called to Confess

As a disciple of Christ who lives with weakness, I want to make an appeal on behalf of the weak. Too many of us die in our weakness—we don't live long enough to reach maturity—and we can't grow if we're dead!

If, when you finish this discussion, you think I think weakness is a desirable thing, I've misled you or you haven't listened well. If you think I think sin is anything other than a brutal parasite that needs to be hunted down and killed, without mercy or remorse, I've not made myself clear.

So let's get something out of the way right now—let's agree that we're all against sin! It makes me angry, at times, to hear disciples talk as if they're the only Christians

EIGHT:

The God

Who

Calls

Disciples

♦

222

opposed to sin. I'm glad they're opposed to it, but it irritates me to hear them speak as if they are alone in their opposition.

One Elijah is enough!

Opposition to sin isn't confined to describing it, illustrating it, lamenting the prevalence of it, damning the sight and sound of it—there's more to it than preaching! We oppose sin by getting help for ourselves to outgrow it, and we oppose it by giving help to others to leave it behind. Our vocation in life is to become more and more like God and to help others do the same.

Now that we've established that we're *against* sin and *for* helping ourselves and others to turn from it, let's move one step further. Let's agree that we all—weak and strong alike—need to *confess* our weakness one to another. We are all, all of us, weak. If we wisely risk ourselves one with another, if we follow the words of James to confess our faults one to another, friendship, brotherhood, and sisterhood will flourish in ways we never thought possible.[1] Maybe then, we'll quit hiding behind the masks we so often wear.

If we wisely risk ourselves one with another, friendship, brotherhood, and sisterhood will flourish in ways we never thought possible.

Yes, it's right to call some Christians "strong" and some "weak." It's right because it's biblical and describes what we see and experience. But "weak" and "strong" are relative terms. They are never used biblically to teach that some are weak all the way through and that others are strong in every area. As a general description, "strong" means that the disciple has, by God's grace, brought his behavioral patterns into line with his inner choice of Jesus as Lord and has done it to a better than average degree. "Weak" means that the disciple hasn't yet the strength to align her behavior with her choice; it means that, as yet, the grace of God hasn't accomplished that in her. She is what the word suggests—lacking in strength!

For the strong to confess weakness doesn't make weakness a desirable thing; it doesn't suggest that sin should be glossed over. But it does admit the truth and adds credibility to the strong.

There are no strong who are not weak in some ways! Even the very strong are far beneath their Master in character. Noah, Abraham, Moses, David, Elijah, Hezekiah, Isaiah, Jeremiah, Peter, Paul, and Barnabas were all subject to weakness. We see it in strong men and women who have trouble with a critical spirit, with seeking prominence, with unbridled ambition, with pride and arrogance, with smugness, mercilessness, or some such thing.

And we see it in ourselves! Have you ever been at an utter loss to explain how you descended to some cheap behavior or speech? Have you ever done something so mean and dishonorable that you felt you were seeing yourself for the first time? Many of us have. With his head hanging in shame, a man I know said, "I didn't know I could do a thing like that." His wrong had not only been a wrong—it was a revelation!

Two boys were wrestling in a school yard many years ago. It was a long, hard tussle, but finally, the bigger boy came out on top and pinned his opponent to the ground. Panting and disappointed, the smaller one said, "You wouldn't have beaten me if I got soup every day like you

EIGHT:

The God

Who

Calls

Disciples

♦

224

do." The bigger boy was Albert Schweitzer, and he never forgot what the smaller boy said.

It's too easy to compare ourselves favorably with others. Who can say how great the advantages and disadvantages in peoples' lives are? When dealing with those caught red-handed in sin, Paul said we are to help restore them and, in that way, help them bear their burdens. But it is to be done in gentleness and without a superior air, for, he said, "each one should carry his own load."[2] Because I could carry your load easily gives me no reason to despise you. Are my blessings greater? Have I been greatly advantaged through life? Have I been getting "soup" every day while you've gone hungry? Let's test our strength against our blessings and maybe we'll not feel so smug about our performance. And maybe we'll learn to openly confess our weakness.

✦

Called to Treat Transgressors Tenderly

How we treat transgressors is critically important! Some poor disciples know no better than to strip the skin right off the sinner's body, leaving him a mass of exposed nerve endings, writhing in pain at even the slightest breath of criticism. They think the sinner must be stripped naked of dignity and subjected to cross-questioning "so he can see the full weight of his sin" (of course!). They're afraid he might be sorry "only because he was caught" rather than *truly* repentant. So the copious tears are ignored, the face burning with shame is dismissed, and his fellow sinners pitilessly drive home the horror of his sin.

EIGHT:

The God

Who

Calls

Disciples

♦

226

And should it happen that he's been guilty before, they feel compelled to remind him that this isn't the first offense (as if he didn't know). They must be sure that this weeping, broken, and shamed sinner knows his wrong is really wrong.

All of this, and we wonder why the fallen and falling don't come to us "spiritual" people for help when they're drowning? They look at themselves each morning in the mirror, these sensitive Christians who are plagued by some evil, they look at themselves and learn to despise the faces they see. "When are you going to grow up, you hypocrite?" they snarl at their reflections. "Why can't you behave like every other decent person?"

Let's suppose one of these struggling souls feeds on pornography (which is so much filthier than sly gossip or subtle self-promotion, don't you know). He thinks that confessing it to anyone would be near impossible, but the shame is destroying him. So in desperation, he approaches Harry, the gentlest man he knows, wanting to share the burden and get help and healing.

Some disciples strip the skin right off the sinner's body, leaving him a mass of exposed nerve endings.

"Well, Harry, what about this porn business? Real slop isn't it? Makes you wonder."

Harry quickly agrees and adds with conviction: "Anyone who reads that filth is a pervert. He ought to see a psychiatrist." Harry goes on to cite statistics on child-molestation, rape, and the like before quoting Jude 8 and the word about "filthy dreamers."

Harry's speaking in the abstract; he doesn't know he's speaking to a porn reader who is dying in his sinful shame.

And will our friend now confess to Harry that he finds sexual excitement in the trash? Never! He was ashamed of it *before* he went to Harry; now he feels worse. He now knows beyond doubt that his self-despising is well grounded. Harry has done two things to our friend, our brother, our fellow disciple: he has made him even more a prisoner to self-loathing, and he has made him afraid to risk himself with anyone else.

Self-loathing paralyzes the heart and destroys any hope of healing. And if the gentle Harry couldn't understand such sinning, how could anyone else? The sinner is driven into further isolation—which is the last thing he needs.

Harry doesn't see him as often as he used to, but when he sees him and asks how he's doing, he always gets the same answer—"Terrific, thanks. If it gets any better I won't be able to stand it"—and the same practiced smile. Off the smiling sinner goes—to his eventual death!

Too ashamed to confess his shame, too self-despising to get his mind on lovely things so he can grow, too lonely to go it alone, too weak to beat it by himself, and too afraid to reveal it to the strong, who might think him a hypocrite. ("Can you imagine him creeping around reading that filth?" he can hear them saying if the word gets out.)

So the weakling capitulates and dies!

As long as he professes to be a Christian, a certain lifestyle is expected of him; but if he quits, he thinks, he won't have to bear that burden. And when the strong, to their surprise, hear he has fallen away—"He was doing so well," they tell each other—when they hear he's fallen away, they go to restore him; but they never get to the

Called to

Treat

Transgressors

Tenderly

♦

227

EIGHT:

The God

Who

Calls

Disciples

◆

228

bottom of his problem. He makes up all kinds of lame excuses for his quitting—nothing that makes sense. They deal with the issues he raises, thinking they are in touch with his need, when the truth is, he's just blowing smoke because he can't bear to name the real problem.

It isn't just that he's now away; it's worse than that! He won't come back! He won't come back because loneliness, weariness, and the great burden of the shame are too much for him. He would only be going back to the same thing!

Let our irreligious critics say what they will; we have no option as Christians but to side with God against sin. Just the same, we need to ask for the grace and wisdom to condemn sin in such a way that we don't make it virtually impossible for a sinner to own up to it. We need to remember that, without knowing it, we may be speaking to someone who is crumbing under a load of guilt.

He's weak, but he isn't a rebel. He isn't the enemy!

I know we'd rather that our brothers and sisters had no weaknesses, but that isn't how it is. Let me ask you this: Would you rather that the weak hide their anguish and awful need or come to someone strong for help in overcoming? Wouldn't you rather they ask for help than burn in their shame? Sure you would!

I don't mean we shouldn't plainly denounce sin—we should! But to lump the struggling disciple with the impenitent clods outside of Christ is a mark of stupidity!

✦

Called to Compassion

We owe it to one another to call each other to maturity; but we mustn't pretend we know each other very well.

To know a person means more than knowing his sin. You have to know the strength of the temptation *as he feels it*—not as you feel it. To know a person means more than knowing that she "gave in." You have to know how hard she tried not to give in. To know a person means more than knowing how often he failed. You have to know how often he succeeded and resisted *before* he failed. To know a person is knowing more than her accomplishments. You have to know how much effort her accomplishments cost. (How *do* you weigh a person's

EIGHT:

The God

Who

Calls

Disciples

♦

230

ability and achievement against her effort?) To know a person is to know more than that his life hangs together well. You have to know if that "holding together" is the result of inner strength or external props. (How do you know what you'd be without the "props" of friends, family, health, and the like?)

There are few judgments more shallow than those which take only *deeds* into account. Some Pharisees thrived on deeds. They prayed, attended church, fasted, tirelessly evangelized, studied the Bible, avoided immorality, and gave money to the poor. *Yet Christ judged them heartless!*

To make no distinction between a person in Christ who struggles against sin—who laments it, hates it, and seeks its destruction—and the Christ-rejecting degenerate who makes no bones about his rejection of God—to make no distinction between these is criminal!

A man who comes to Christ out of a really horrible moral background brings with him a lot of trash that he has renounced in the name of Christ his Lord. It's renounced, but it's entwined in and around him as an intruder and a parasite. It will take time, patience, accountability, help, and prayer to remove it. God doesn't work "moral miracles," even though we often wish he would. People are nurtured in evil, they are shaped by it, and it becomes part of their emotional, mental, and social makeup. They aren't healed in an instant!

To know people is to know more than *what* they do. It's to know *why they do what they do and what they would do if they had the power to do it.*

"To the weak I became weak, to win the weak. I have become all things to all men so that by all possible means I might save some."

—1 Corinthians 9:22

✦

Called to Befriend Sinners

Strength isn't given to the strong so they can strut! First Corinthians 12:7 says the gifts of God are given "for the common good." God strengthens people, in part, so they can help the weak.

Power used for personal aggrandizement is pagan power. There is to be no display of it—no flexing of spiritual muscles, no inter-congregational contests to discover "Mr. or Ms. Mature of the Brotherhood." Strength is no personal gift to be consumed by the individual who has it.

The apostle Paul was one of God's really strong men, yet he was keenly sensitive to the weak and calls us to be

EIGHT:

The God

Who

Calls

Disciples

♦

232

the same. Through his words, we get a view of God's philosophy on strength.

> We who are strong ought to bear with the failings of the weak and not to please ourselves. Each of us should please his neighbor for his good, to build him up. For even Christ did not please himself.[1]

> And we urge you, brothers, warn those who are idle, encourage the timid, help the weak, be patient with everyone.[2]

> To the weak I became weak, to win the weak. I have become all things to all men so that by all possible means I might save some.[3]

> Who is weak, and I do not feel weak? Who is led into sin, and I do not inwardly burn?[4]

> Be careful, however, that the exercise of your freedom does not become a stumbling block to the weak. . . . Won't he be emboldened to eat what has been sacrificed to idols? So this weak brother, for whom Christ died, is destroyed by your knowledge. When you sin against your brothers in this way and wound their weak conscience, you sin against Christ.[5]

Ask Paul, "How do you feel about the weak?" and reflect on the many things he has said and implied about them in these few texts. Ask him if he thinks they're worth the trouble.

Ask yourself what you think of them. Go ahead, just let your mind settle on some weak and struggling disciple you know. Now, in light of what we've heard from God, in light of what he has been to us, what is our obligation to these fellow strugglers?

Picture this: Three disciples go to the house of an unbeliever to eat, and the host sets meat before them. One of the brothers is weak in his appropriation of the freedom and light that Jesus has brought, so he inquires where the host got the meat. He learns it is the leftovers from idolatrous worship, so he can't eat it and says so.

The second disciple knows better. He has more fully grasped truth as it is found in Christ, and with a snort at the other's ignorance, he tears into his piece of meat, cackling as he goes.

The third disciple is Paul. He could go ahead and eat, because he knows the meat is neutral. He could refuse to eat, while chiding his weak brother for his ignorance: "If it wasn't for this poor ignorant brother, I would gladly eat your meat, my dear sir," he could have said. Or he could abstain from eating and take his place (without a sermon) with his weak brother. He, too, would become the butt of the jokes from disciple number two and an object of scorn to the pagan host. Paul would be glad to do it. He holds his brother to be a cheerful burden, and the brother's burden becomes his burden.

The strong and those of reputation are often afraid to befriend someone with real struggles in the moral arena. They fear for their own names. They don't wish to be thought of as endorsing sinful behavior, of "being soft" on sin. They must protect their names so they won't lose influence with others (for the work's sake, don't you understand). This leads to the isolation of the struggler from the very people he needs.

Parker Henderson is a friend of mine and a strong, upright man of God. Once, when a number of us were dealing with a transgressor, this strong, righteous man became as tender as a mother with her child and stood by the one who sat in shame. None of us was mistreating the sinner; we were seeking his highest good. It's just that Parker unashamedly moved to his side, spoke gently to him, and then spoke for him. I won't ever forget that.

How many blameless men and women do you know who are known as the sinner's friend? We know those who are evangelists, teachers, scholars, givers, speakers, and leaders; but how many do you know who are immediately identified as a friend of sinners?

We owe these people!

♦

✦

Called to Respect Repentance

How do you know what's in a person's heart? First Corinthians 2:11 says you can't unless that person tells you. "But surely behavior must tell us something," someone protests. It certainly does, but how much does it tell us?

Jesus makes a mind-boggling statement in Luke 22. The disciples are brawling about position, about who was the best of them, and they were doing all this on the night they betrayed Christ! They had shown themselves spiritually out of tune, self-serving, quarrelsome, and selfish, and here the Master says of them, "You are those who have stood by me in my trials." How could he say that? How could he say that of them?

235

EIGHT:

The God

Who

Calls

Disciples

♦

236

He could say that because behind their actual performance, he saw their hearts, saw what they would do if they could only execute it, saw what they cherished and dreamed about, saw them stand by him as well as they could! He never for a moment doubted their genuineness! But we, sometimes, are tempted to doubt the genuineness of our brothers' and sisters' repentance.

We're tempted to doubt the genuineness of another because of the repeated nature of the wrongs. *Once* we don't mind, *twice* we raise our eyebrows, and *three* times we begin to talk of impenitence. We feel this temptation more strongly if the sin is against *us*.

We hurt our own husbands, wives, children, family, and friends repeatedly, but we don't doubt our *own* genuineness before God. We know what we cherish in our hearts toward God and man, so we strive by God's grace to amend our lives, and we dismiss the arithmetic (was it once, twice, or a score of times?). We hurt our family and friends repeatedly, but we don't doubt our love for them. There's more to impenitence than mere arithmetic, and there's more to goodness or badness than a set of figures.

Behind their actual performance, he saw what they would do if they could only execute it.

We're tempted to doubt the genuineness of another because of our human limitations. We can't see into peoples' hearts, you see, so we foolishly judge the outward act as if it were the whole story. If we're sinned against, and sinned against repeatedly, we have neither the time nor the desire to wonder about motivations.

We can and must judge acts as evil when they're clearly evil, but we mustn't pretend we know anything about the deep roots of an act, the motivations (plural) of behavior. That's part of the reason Jesus warns us against censoriousness and the lack of mercy.[1] We can't get inside the heads of people, so we judge simply on the basis of actual deeds or words. This is perfectly legitimate within bounds, but the bounds are real—even if we choose to ignore them.

We can examine our own motivations for our evil (though even that's definitely limited); and while we condemn our wicked thoughts and deeds, we still believe we are sincere Christians. What we grant to ourselves we find difficult to extend to others, because we can't know their inner feelings.

We're tempted to doubt the genuineness of another because we have no personal and emotional commitment to that person. If you've done me wrong, a painful wrong, and I have no emotional padding to absorb that pain, I will tend to treat the wrong as a legal violation with nothing to soften it—this is not the love that "covers a multitude of sins."

The father and older brother in Luke 15 both had the same information about the younger boy. The older son thought the father wasn't taking the other boy's wickedness seriously. Surely, if the father had a clearer view of wickedness, he wouldn't be so lenient. That was part of what the older boy thought, but he was wrong.

He saw sin in the abstract; the father saw it in the concrete. The son saw it as a violation of God's law; the father saw it as that and more! He saw it as a destructive force, as something that had been devouring one he loved. To the father it was a personal heartbreak, and when the younger son showed up, the father had a vested interest in believing the genuineness of the recovery. The father

EIGHT:

The God

Who

Calls

Disciples

♦

238

hated all wrongdoing, but he hated his boy's because of what it was doing to the child he so loved. Love made the father want to believe in the young man's genuineness.

The longer I live, the more I see this truth: If you have a personal and vital interest in another, you give him or her all kinds of credit. Paul says love doesn't keep a record of sins, and Peter says it covers over a multitude of sins. There's more than pardon involved in all this. When you've made a personal commitment to someone, you not only pardon his or her wrongs, you find many of them irrelevant to your relationship.

I don't mean they cease to be wrongs! I mean they cease to be a threat to your relationship. Lovers simply refuse to take note of every offense. Yes, lovers often confront one another—they must at times—but more often than not, they refuse to make an issue of the multitude of "lower level" wrongs. They view them as "sins within the covenant." They know that such sins don't really reflect the commitment the other feels for their relationship.

We live this way with our families. Do you take your wife or husband to task for every discourtesy? Do you always "settle it" with some family member who is abrupt or unkind? Thank God, we let hundreds of wrongs pass without making a drama out of them. Thank God, we live with one another under the shelter of a loving commitment that covers over a multitude of sins.

If the sins are major-league issues, why of course they must be dealt with! But we shouldn't feel uneasy about our willingness to let the bulk of them slide. When we're too good at detecting the wrongs of another, especially if they're against us, maybe we're too sensitive to our "rights," and maybe we need to invest some emotional commitment in that person.

We're tempted to doubt the genuineness of another when the sin is outrageous. If we are people of blameless behavior (that doesn't mean sinless!), we look on the more flagrant sins with disbelief. Homosexuality, molesting children, major-league embezzlement, and the like simply astonish us. The more morally correct we are, the more we're tempted to believe a genuine disciple couldn't do such a thing.

There's no point in denying that some sins are more heinous than others. Precisely what makes one more abominable than another is a discussion for another time, but it's more than the "simple act." In any case, we all feel sure we know that some are worse than others, and the more callous and outrageous the sin, the more certain we are that the perpetrator can't be a genuine Christian.

A tortured young man came into my home one evening a long time ago. After a long silence he said, "Jim, all my life I've felt the tendency toward homosexual behavior, and for the very first time, last week, I got involved in it." He couldn't go on.

If he were my son, I'd be frantic; but I wouldn't leave him to fight it out alone, and I wouldn't doubt his longing to experience holy freedom!

When I asked if I needed to read to him from Romans 1 to show his behavior to be sinful, he said, "I know better than you'll ever know how wicked it is. You read about it; I live with it." He was in agony.

Did this young man sin? Yes! If he were my son, I'd be frantic. I'd weep, beg, rebuke, and maybe even scream. I'd quote texts, and I'd try to scare it out of him; but I wouldn't leave him to fight it out alone, and I wouldn't doubt his longing to experience holy freedom!

I'm not suggesting that you silence God's call to honorable living. It isn't kindness that leaves people wallowing in their weakness because we're "too loving" to confront. Say that sin is sin; don't get sentimental over wickedness. Take whatever steps you have to, to keep your brothers and sisters from repeatedly hurting you or others, but don't judge their hidden recesses. Take their word for it that they are struggling against the evil.

♦

> *"Carry each other's burdens, and in this way you*
> *will fulfill the law of Christ."*
>
> —Galatians 6:2

◆

Called to Carry the Weak

The tiring truth is that we weaklings are demanding. If you go out, in the name of Christ, to call the weak and the needy, we'll turn up—weak and in need! If you don't want us, don't call us!

We have no right to sulk, but we do; we wish we were through with our sin, but we aren't; we'd like to be able to stand on God's grace without having to continuously lean on you, but we can't right now. We came because you called us in the name of God, and we believed the good news. Sometimes people act as though the invitation for us weak and needy people to come to Christ dissolves our needs—but it doesn't! We come, weak and needy!

EIGHT:

The God

Who

Calls

Disciples

♦

242

But many in the church want *winners*—self-motivated, go-getters who can run for miles on a glass of water and an occasional smile of appreciation—people who show no signs of fatigue, and if they do, they refuse our help with a pained grin and plough on.

To bet only on winners or on those who give you reason to believe they soon will be winners is pagan! To choose only those who cannot burden you is unlike Christ. To choose only those who can help you is to be an exploiter, a taker.

The "burden" of the weak is felt especially by ministers and other leaders who are trying to "glorify God through the growth of a big church." These leaders are usually the ones who think up the programs to make the church grow, they are the ones who try to involve everyone in these programs, and they're the ones who get mad when the weak ones won't get involved.

If you go out, in the name of Christ, to call the weak and the needy, we'll turn up—weak and in need!

Salaried ministers and public leaders have a special interest in seeing the church grow. Growth justifies their salaries and demonstrates their effectiveness. Personal identities are on the line. If the assembly doesn't grow, the leadership feels the pressure.

But the church is not a stage on which the strong "do their thing." It isn't the minister's chariot on which he rides from glory to greater glory; it isn't an instrument through which the leaders minister to God. It is a body of people to whom they are to minister for God. These brothers and sisters are not a program. People rightly resent being used by anybody. They don't like being used by prime-time television evangelists who build monuments to themselves and beg hard-working people to sustain their opulent lifestyle; and they don't like being used by fired-up ministers and leaders who are pursuing personal agendas.

Listen to this from Dietrich Bonhoeffer: "It is only when he is a burden that another person is really a brother and not merely an object to be manipulated."[1] It's only when I feel a responsibility toward my brothers and sisters as my burdens to bear that they cease to be tools for my schemes. If I view them as burdens, I can't view them as toys or pawns to play with or use. To patch them up just so they can help me fulfill my dreams or my projects—my "destiny"—to do that is to make tools out of them! To make their burdens mine—to make them my burdens—and to carry them is to fulfill the law of Christ.

> *"Each one should use whatever gift he has received to serve others, faithfully administering God's grace in its various forms."*
>
> —1 Peter 4:10

◆

Called to Serve

Like every other dimension of the disciple's call, the call to serve is to be rooted in the pursuit of Christ-likeness. In John 13 the Master washed the feet of the apostolic group and said, "Now that I, your Lord and Teacher, have washed your feet, you also should wash one another's feet."

This beautiful act of service was a demonstration of *acceptance.* In washing the apostles' feet, Jesus claimed them as his own. And so when we serve another, we demonstrate our loving acceptance of them as part of us. As disciples of Christ, we are called to *serve.*

We're called to serve where we can. There. Serve there! Wherever you are right now. Another day may find you

EIGHT:

The God

Who

Calls

Disciples

♦

246

half way around the world. Today finds you where you are; serve there. Another year may find you in the middle of some trackless jungle or some urban ghetto ministering to ignorant or oppressed people. Thank God! But for now, serve in your home, your apartment complex, on the job, in the park—wherever. Serve *where* you can.

We are called to serve when we can. "He gives twice who gives quickly" is a proverb that has earned its place in memory. The trouble with a lot of our lovely plans to help people is that they assume the people will be around long enough for us to fulfill them. If you have the strength to serve, do it now. Don't wait; the opportunity may not return. When you miss an opportunity, don't live in agony, grinding on it. Dismiss it and go on.

We're called to serve how we can. Yes, I know you'd like to have his or her talents. I know! I've met such people. They fill you with jealousy—sometimes godly, sometimes not. Ah, well. Give what you've got. Give what God has given you to give.

Christ speaks of giving a cup of cold water in his name, but sometimes we're tempted to think that's just a concession to the losers.

Christ speaks of giving a cup of cold water in his name, but sometimes we're tempted to think that's just a concession to the losers. Your Master doesn't talk that way, and such phrases didn't find their way into the deathless Word of God for us to dismiss them as trivia.

Can you kill a prejudice against Christians by showing a genuine interest in the lives of non-Christians? Can you baby-sit for a young couple while they go to the movies or the park for a needed break? Can you mow a lawn and leave another Christian free to teach a Bible class? Can you make people feel warm and wanted in your home? Can you read to children or to older folks who can't see well?

Can you raise two or three children in a home where Christ is Lord and love is the rule? Can you nobly and gallantly bear your misfortune and, in this way, show people you have an invisible means of support? Can you buy a rose, a ballpoint pen, a tube of lipstick, a tie tack, or some such thing, wrap it in pretty paper, and drop it by with no hoopla? If you can do any of these things, or a host of things like these, you can serve. Serve *how* you can.

We are called to serve as wisely as we can. Service covers a lot of ground, but I want to zero in on material help for just a minute. Sometimes we're asked for money and we aren't sure whether the money will be used to feed an addiction or a family. It can't be right to suspend judgment forever, but it doesn't help those who need help if the money (or whatever) is wasted, or worse. Someone said, "Intelligent giving and intelligent withholding are alike true charity."

To bring people within the circle of our influence and fellowship is one way to enable us to *really* help. To restore family units or church ties by giving things other than food and clothing is wise service.

I can't carry this very far, but Christians and churches would do well to sit down and work out a policy under God by which they can serve people who are in need. We all know that it takes more than a shed filled with clothes and canned goods to do effective benevolence. Since it is part of our submission to Christ, it merits close attention, thought, and prayer. "Benevolent bungling" helps no one. Serve as *wisely* as you can.

EIGHT:

The God

Who

Calls

Disciples

♦

248

We are called to serve who we can. Some people are hungry and need food, some are lonely and need company, some are jobless and need work, some are frightened and need assurance, some are rejected and need acceptance, some are utterly undisciplined and need firm guidance—they all have one thing in common, they *need;* and we are called to serve.

As I've said, help must be wisely given if it is to be "help," but we can't forever debate the "worthiness" of people before we lend a helping hand. There are families to think of, and there are some situations that defy debate and suspended judgment—the need is too stark. There is the parable of the "Good Samaritan," and there is Matthew 25.

The fear of being "conned" may lead us to dry our eyes and cut off the needy. But if God waited until *we* were worthy of help, he'd wait for the blue snow. Rejecting needy people on the grounds of some theory might bring us face to face with God on the wrong side of Matthew 25.

We are called to serve without broadcasting it. I don't mean we should never share our serving experiences. That'd be a real loss, at times. I do mean that a little sharing goes a long way. There are not many things more tedious and repelling than someone going on about their acts of service. If they are to be made known, God can work it out—someone will spread the word about the service rendered.

A friend of mine is a CPA. We were discussing two other friends who were extremely liberal with their wealth. My friend bragged on them both and said of one in particular, "He's one of those people who can live without applause!" I loved that remark.

"If anyone would come after me, he must deny himself
and take up his cross daily and follow me."

—Luke 9:23

✦

Called to Deny Self

If anyone would come after me, he must deny himself and take up his cross daily and follow me.[1]

If anyone comes to me and does not hate his father and mother, his wife and children, his brothers and sisters—yes, even his own life—he cannot be my disciple. And anyone who does not carry his cross and follow me cannot be my disciple. . . . In the same way, any of you who does not give up everything he has cannot be my disciple.[2]

What am I to do with these texts? What should I say about these words the Master uttered so soberly?

EIGHT:

The God

Who

Calls

Disciples

♦

250

Yes, I know there are a lot of things they don't mean, but they do mean something! And shouldn't I conclude that they're fundamentally important since three times he said, "If you won't do this, you can't be my disciple"?

Because in some quarters self-denial is an odious subject, are we to dismiss as nothing the call of Christ? Are we to empty the lordship of Christ of authority because some people have paganized that truth? Let's forget the perversion and the foolishness and face his demand on our lives.

When he speaks of "self-denial," Christ speaks of our receiving him as Lord and dethroning ourselves. We're not permitted to play God! Self-denial is that inner choice, that heartfelt purpose to make Jesus Lord of all. There is nothing vague about it. The man rises up within himself and by the grace of God says, "I've exalted myself long enough! I've pursued my own will long enough! No more! I do here gladly and soberly surrender myself and all that is mine to him." That is self-denial as Jesus speaks of it.

We don't have to understand all that's involved in choosing Christ in order to choose him.

To make Jesus Lord is to deny that lordship to anyone or anything else. Those closest to us—fathers, mothers, brothers, sisters, husbands, wives, children, friends—all are to be rejected as lords. No man, no group of men, no creed, no commitment can take his place! As there is one God, one faith, and one baptism, there is also one Lord. Where his commands stop, there are no more. No relationship, however cherished, is exempt from that imperial command. Those who refuse Christ as Lord for love of family or any other love cannot be his disciples.

That inner, utter surrender of ourselves to Christ becomes the foundation on which our lives are shaped. We can't affirm that choice without intending to pursue the will of Christ. We don't have to understand all that's involved in this choosing of Christ. The apostles didn't, but they made their choice and learned as they went. The young man who signs up for the Marines may not be prepared for the tormentor who wears three stripes, but he's in and lives with his commitment.

In all of this, we're talking about people who make one central choice and are willing to pay the price for that choice. Of course self-denial sometimes requires us to say "no" to things, but is that unusual? Athletes grunt and sweat their way through hours of work day after day to reach the top of their profession. Swimmers, musicians, scientists, doctors, and all kinds of people make a central choice and stick to it—and they pay the price that comes with it.

"Self-denial" has a bad ring to it. The word has been so abused that it conjures up the image of people who run around in a fever and look as though they have a permanent case of indigestion. "Self-denial," Fosdick said, "is not negative repression, but the cost of positive achievement."[3] When Christ spoke of counting the cost, it wasn't with a view to *losing* something but to *gaining* something. In one of his parables, a merchant saw a matchless pearl and just had to have it and sold all he had to buy it.[4] Jesus is not teaching that the man *lost* his wealth when he sold all to get it; but that he *gained* something of much greater value.

EIGHT:

The God

Who

Calls

Disciples

♦

252

Do we lose ourselves when we spend our lives in lovely toil on behalf of the unloved and the unlovely? Or do we not lose ourselves when we live a life of utter selfishness? Who sacrificed himself—the drunken victim of venereal disease or the young man who has, for Christ's sake and for the sake of his family, kept himself from dishonor?

Denying ourselves gossip just might result in being blessed with friends. Keeping ourselves from idols will, in Christ, result in our knowing and loving the living God—and knowing God is life everlasting! No, we're not to do right just to "get a reward," but it's still true that to do evil is to sacrifice oneself, while to pursue goodness, in the name of Christ, is to find life abundant.

When Christ spoke of counting the cost, it wasn't with a view to *losing* something but to *gaining* something.

∽

And when this life is over and we go home to live forever with the Master, we'll be glad we lived "sacrificially." We'll regret no effort we made to draw someone to Jesus Christ. We'll know no remorse over the pain and insult we endured on behalf of the unloved and the unlovely. And should someone there say that we sacrificed much on earth, we'll protest. We'll be glad that we renounced every hint of pride, every whisper of arrogance, every whiff of selfishness. We'll rejoice that, despite the fact that such things found a place in us while we lived here on earth, they never found a home. We'll rejoice eternally that we chose, with a deliberate choice, to cast ourselves from the throne and place Jesus Christ there as Lord!

Notes

Introduction
1. Exod. 33:17–23.
2. Colin Morris, *The Word About Words* (New York: Abingdon Press, 1975), 27.
3. C. S. Lewis, *The Lion, the Witch, and the Wardrobe* (New York: Collier Books, 1970).
4. *Inspiring Quotations,* compiled by A. M. Wells (n.p., 1988), 47.
5. Howard Butt, *The Velvet Covered Brick* (New York: Harper & Row, 1973), 14.
6. Harry E. Fosdick, *Riverside Sermons* (New York: Harper & Row, 1958), 270.

Chapter One: THE GOD WHO LOVES HUMANS
A Vulnerable God
1. Isa. 6:5.
2. W. M. Clow, *The Cross in Christian Experience* (London: Hodder & Stoughton, 1908), 51.

Why Would He Bother?
1. John 1:14; Phil. 2:8.
2. E. Stanley Jones, *Victory through Surrender* (Nashville: Abingdon Press, 1966; Apex Edition, 1971), 51.
3. R. L. Stevenson, "Exodus," in *The Speakers Bible,* ed. John Hastings, 18 vols. (Grand Rapids, Mich.: Baker Book House, 1978), 1:76.
4. P. T. Forsyth, *God the Holy Father* (London: Independent Press Ltd., 1957).

God's Loving Purpose

1. R. A. Varghese, ed., *The Intellectuals Speak Out about God* (Dallas: Gateway, 1984), 23–27.

2. Bertrand Russell, *Mysticism and Logic: And Other Essays,* 10th imp. (London: Allen & Unwen, 1951), 47–48.

3. Col. 1:15–23.

Cherishing the Mystery

1. Robert Davidson, *Wisdom and Worship* (London: SCM Press, 1990).

2. Joseph Parker, *Preaching through the Bible,* 14 vols. (n.p.: Baker Book House), 11:294.

3. *Sing to the Lord* (Kansas City, Mo.: Lillenas Publishing Co., 1993), 228.

4. J. H. Jowett, *The School of Calvary* (London: James Clarke & Co., 1910), 18–19.

Don't Give Up On Me!

1. 1 John 4:14, 16.

This God Came to Die!

1. Matt. 20:28, author paraphrase.

2. 1 John 4:9.

3. 1 John 3:16 MOFFATT.

Love in Four Dimensions

1. Eph. 3:19.

2. Eph. 3:18, emphasis added.

3. John 3:16, emphasis added.

4. Clow, *The Cross in Christian Experience,* 57.

5. Rom. 8:32.

6. Rom. 5:5.

7. Gal. 5:16–26.

8. C. S. Lewis, *The Problem of Pain* (London: The Centenary Press, 1941), 36–37.

9. 2 Cor. 5:14, author paraphrase.

A Love That Will Not Let Me Go

1. "The Garden of Prosperine," *The Oxford Book of Death* (Oxford: Oxford Univ. Press, 1983), 162.

2. Charles Dickens, *A Tale of Two Cities* (London: Heron Books, 1967), 172–73.

3. James S. Stewart, *King For Ever* (Nashville: Abingdon Press, 1975), 111–12.

4. Matt. 10:34.

The Death of Death

1. *The Expositor's Bible*, 6 vols. (Grand Rapids, Mich.: Eerdmans, 1956), 4:528.

2. Eph. 2:3.

3. See John 1:4–5.

4. Eph. 2:4.

5. Eph. 2:4–5.

6. Heb. 11:1; Heb. 4:3.

7. Heb. 2:14.

♦

Chapter Two: THE GOD WHO LOVES THE WEAK

Allowances

1. Rom. 5:6.

2. Col. 1:28; Heb. 13:20–21.

3. *A Book on Friendship* (Kansas City, Mo.: Hallmark Cards, Inc., 1977), 11.

4. Rom. 15:1.

Bruised Reeds and Smoking Wicks

1. Isa. 42:1–4.

2. Matt. 12:18–21.

3. 2 Tim. 2:23–26, especially v. 24.

4. Ezek. 40:3; Ezek. 29:6–7; 2 Kings 18:21.

5. Acts 10:38.

Receiver of Wrecks

1. Luke 15:1–2.

2. Marcus Dodds, *Christ and Man* (London: Hodder & Stoughton, 1909), 38.

3. Matt. 11:28–30.

The Shepherd King

1. Isa. 40:9–11.

Where Are the Stretchers?

1. Ezek. 34:2–10, especially vv. 2–6.

2. Parker, *Preaching through the Bible,* 8:305–6.

3. Mike Yaconelli, "Evangelico Gigilo," *The Wittenburg Door,* no. 55 (June/July 1980).

4. Matt. 25:41–46, author paraphrase.

Chapter Three: THE GOD WHO IS HOLY

A Love That Can Be Trusted

1. Cf. 1 John 1:9.

God's Ethical Holiness

1. Lev. 19:2 KJV.
2. Exod. 15:11.
3. Hab. 1:13.
4. Lev. 17–26.
5. Ps. 25:8–9.
6. Ps. 24:3–4, 6 MOFFATT.
7. Gen. 18:25.
8. Ps. 96:10–13.
9. 1 John 1:9.
10. Rom. 3:21–6.
11. Rom. 4:25; Rom. 8:32.

More Than Pardon

1. Matt. 5:6.
2. 1 Thess. 5:23–24.

The Gift of Holiness

1. Col. 1:19–20.
2. Acts 18:27.
3. Acts 11:18; 2 Tim. 2:25.
4. Phil. 2:13; Heb. 13:20–21.
5. Gal. 2:16.
6. Exod. 31:13.
7. Lev. 20:8.
8. Eph. 5:25–26.
9. Heb. 13:12.
10. Cf. Exod. 19:5–6; 1 Pet. 2:5–9.
11. Heb. 10:10.
12. 2 Cor. 3:18; Rom. 12:2.
13. 1 Cor. 1:8–9.
14. 1 Cor. 4:7.

"And Maddest of All . . ."
1. Cervantes, *Don Quixote, the Man of La Mancha.*
2. Heb. 11:16.

Chapter Four: THE GOD WHO FORGIVES SINS

Forgiveness and Repentance
1. Robert Mackintosh, *Christianity and Sin* (London: Duckworth & Co., 1913), 183.
2. Ps. 51:17.
3. R. Mackintosh, *Christianity and Sin,* 184.
4. This seems to be the point of Matthew 18:10–35.
5. Luke 13:3.

If Our Hearts Condemn Us
1. H. B. Swete, *The Forgiveness of Sins* (London: Macmillan & Co., Ltd., 1917), 177.
2. Cf. Rom. 5:1.
3. 1 John 3:19–21 PHILLIPS.

Isn't Somebody Going to Forgive Me?
1. James Moffatt, *His Gifts and His Promises* (Edinburgh: T & T Clark, 1934), 88–89.
2. Forsyth, *God the Holy Father,* 17–19.

Of Judges and Friends
1. Matt. 5:29–30.
2. Hugh Mackintosh, *The Highway of God* (Edinburgh: T & T Clark, 1931), 79.
3. John 15:14; Isa. 41:8.
4. H. Mackintosh, *The Highway of God,* 80.
5. Ps. 130:4.

Ruby Bridges
1. See *The Moral Life of Children,* and *Children of Crisis* for complete story.

Humans Need Forgiving
1. L. E. Maxwell, *Crowded to Christ* (Chicago: Moody Press, 1976).

God Delights in Forgiving!
1. Isa. 55:1–7.
2. Isa. 55:7 JB.
3. Matt. 18.
4. Mic. 7:18–20 PHILLIPS, emphasis added.

No Fishing!
1. Horatio G. Spafford, *It Is Well with My Soul,* in *Songs of Faith and Praise* (West Monroe, La.: Howard Publishing Co.), 490.
2. 1 John 1.
3. *The Complete Poetry and Selected Prose of John Donne* (Toronto: Random House, 1952), 270–71.
4. Jer. 31:34.
5. Heb. 10:12–14.
6. Isa. 43:25.
7. Wilbur Rees, *$3 Worth of God* (Valley Forge, Penn.: Judson Press, 1971), 28.

Why Must You Die?
1. John 3:17.
2. Ibid.

Chapter Five: THE GOD OF THE TOWEL

Twelve Lords, One Servant
1. John 10:18.
2. Matt. 17:5b.
3. Phil. 2:5–11, emphasis added.

God Is Not Slumming
1. Rees, *$3 Worth of God,* 83.

With Love and Forethought
1. John 13:1.
2. John 12:27; 13:1.
3. John 13:3.
4. Ibid.
5. Ibid.

The Lamb at the Center of the Throne
1. John 18:36.

2. John 17:2; Matt. 28:18.
3. Rev. 1:5; 17:17; Ps. 2:8; Eph. 1:20–22.
4. Will Durant, *Christ and Caesar* (New York: Simon and Schuster, 1972), 670.
5. G. C. Berkouwer, *Faith and Sanctification* (Grand Rapids, Mich.: Eerdmans, 1977), 142.

Power: Pagan and Christ-like
1. Matt. 20:25.
2. Matt. 20:25–28 NRSV.

"Made a Difference to That One"
1. *Chicken Soup for the Soul,* written and compiled by Jack Canfield and Mark Victor Hansen (Deerfield Beach, Fla.: Health Communications, Inc., 1993), 22–23.

Take My Word for It
1. John 14:9.
2. John 14:7.
3. John 14:11.
4. Ibid.
5. Matt. 11:29.

Only Half the Cure
1. Luke 9:38–43.
2. Luke 9:44.
3. Luke 9:45.
4. Paul Scherer, *The Word of God Sent* (Grand Rapids, Mich.: Baker Book House, 1977), 173.

Chapter Six: THE GOD WHO ALLOWS SUFFERING
Can You Still Trust Me?
1. Davidson, *Wisdom and Worship,* 173. See also *The Courage to Doubt* (London: SCM Press, 1990), 1.

Bad Fridays and "Good Friday"
1. Francois Mauriac, foreword to *Night,* by Elie Wiesel (New York: Bantom Books, 1986).

Go Tell John
1. Luke 7:19.
2. Luke 7:21–23.

"What Doesn't Destroy Me Makes Me Strong"

1. *Twilight of the Idols* (n.p.: Maxims & Arrows; Penguin, 1990).

2. Harry E. Fosdick, *The Meaning of Faith* (Nashville: Abingdon Press, 1982), 177–78.

3. Acts 10:38 RSV.

The One Who Holds the Knife

1. Russell, *Mysticism and Logic.*

2. Viktor Frankl, *Man's Search for Meaning* (New York: Simon & Schuster, 1984), 46–47.

"It Seemed Good in Thy Sight"

1. Parker, *Preaching through the Bible,* 10:197.

Don't Go through It Alone

1. Arthur Gossip, *The Hero in Thy Soul* (Edinburgh: T & T Clark, 1928), 110.

The Pain God Bears

1. See Luke 13:10–16.

2. Matt. 25:31–46.

3. *The Expositor's Bible,* 4:528.

The Man in the Iron Mask

1. Alexandre Dumas, *The Man in the Iron Mask* (London: Bancroft Books, 1973).

2. A William Bast television adaptation of *The Man in the Iron Mask,* performed by Richard Chamberlin, Patrick McGoohan, and Jenny Agutter.

The Beliefs of Unbelief

1. Paul Roubiczek, *Existentialism—For and Against* (Cambridge: Cambridge University Press, 1966), 125; Jean Paul Sartre, *Words* (Middlesex, England: Penguin Books, 1964).

2. *Objections to Humanism,* contributed to and edited by H. J. Blackham (London: Constable, 1963), 105.

Tractor-Driving, Cow-Scratching John

1. *The Last Thing We Talk About* (Elgin, Ill.: David C. Cook Publishing Co., 1984), 103–4.

"Sent to Me by Heaven"
1. Dickens, *A Tale of Two Cities,* 412–13, 434–35.
2. Heb. 2:14.

Chapter Seven: THE GOD WHO MADE YOKES

Not What They Expected
1. Isa. 53:2.
2. Mark 6:2–3.
3. John 1:27.
4. *The Speaker's Bible,* 11:39.

The Glory of the Ordinary
1. Daniel Poling, *An Adventure in Evangelism* (London: Revell, 1925), 130.

The Sacredness of the Secular
1. Eph. 4:28.
2. Acts 6:2–3.
3. 1 Thess. 2:1–12; Phil. 1:15.
4. Luke 12:13–21.
5. Col. 3:22–24.

Stolen Joy
1. Larry Peabody, *Secular Work Is Full-Time Service* (Ft. Washington, Penn.: Christian Literature Crusade, 1974).
2. Ibid., 57.
3. John R. W. Stott, *Our Guilty Silence* (n.p.: Hodder & Stoughton, 1973), 13.
4. Eph. 4:11.

Chapter Eight: THE GOD WHO CALLS DISCIPLES

Called to Copy God
1. Eph. 4:32.
2. Rom. 15:7.
3. Phil. 2:5 ff.
4. Col. 3:1, 5.
5. 1 Pet. 1:14–15.
6. Deut. 7:7–8; 9:4 ff.

Called to Confess
1. James 5:16.
2. Gal. 6:5.

Called to Befriend Sinners
1. Rom. 15:1–3.
2. 1 Thess. 5:14.
3. 1 Cor. 9:22.
4. 2 Cor. 11:29.
5. 1 Cor. 8:9–12.

Called to Respect Repentance
1. Matt. 7:1–5.

Called to Carry the Weak
1. Dietrich Bonhoeffer, *Life Together* (New York: Harper & Row, 1954).

Called to Deny Self
1. Luke 9:23.
2. Luke 14:26, 33.
3. Harry E. Fosdick, *The Meaning of Service* (Nashville: Abingdon Press, 1983), 92.
4. Matt. 13:45–46.